A REGAL BIBLE COMMENTARY FOR LAYMEN

Winning the Battles of Life

A Life-Related Study in Joshua

Paul E. Toms

GL
Regal Books
A Division of GL Publications
Ventura, California, U.S.A.

Other good Regal reading in this series:
Soulsearch (Ecclesiastes)
　　　by Robert S. Ricker with Ron Pitkin

You Are Loved and Forgiven (Colossians)
　　　by Lloyd John Ogilvie

God with Us (Matthew)
　　　by D.A. Carson

Confronted by Love (2 Corinthians)
　　　by Dan Baumann

Except where otherwise indicated, Scripture quotations in this book are from:
NIV—Holy Bible: The New International Version Copyright © 1978 by The
International Bible Society. Used by permission of Zondervan Bible Publishers.

Also quoted are:
KJV—Authorized King James Version
RSV—Revised Standard Version of the Bible, Copyright 1946 and 1952 by the
Division of the Christian Education of the NCCC, U.S.A., and used by permission.
TLB—The Living Bible, Copyright © 1971 by Tyndale House Publishers,
Wheaton, Illinois. Used by permission.

Published by Regal Books
A Division of GL Publications
Ventura, California 93006
Printed in U.S.A.

Library of Congress Cataloging in Publication Data

Toms, Paul E.
　　This land is your land.

　　(A Bible commentary for laymen)
　　Bibliography: p.
　　1. Bible. O.T. Joshua—Commentaries.　　I. Title.　　II. Series.
BS1295.3.T67　　　1986　　　　　　　　222'.207　　　　　　　　86-15417
ISBN 0-8307-1161-9

2 3 4 5 6 7 8 9 10 / 91 90 89 88 87

Rights for publishing this book in other languages are contracted by Gospel
Literature International (GLINT) foundation. GLINT also provides technical
help for the adaptation, translation, and publishing of Bible study resources
and books in scores of languages worldwide. For further information, contact
GLINT, Post Office Box 488, Rosemead, California, 91770, U.S.A., or the
publisher.

Contents

A coursebook comprising the teacher's manual and reproducible Discovery materials for classes and Bible study groups using this commentary is available from your church supplier.

1
Nothing Succeeds Like Success

Joshua 1

If you could get into a time machine and set the dials for about 1300 B.C., when you got to that time period things would appear drastically different! You would find yourself in the late Bronze Age, about 1,000 years before the early Mayan culture in the Americas, and 600 years before the Etruscans began their move toward Italy.

In Crete there are great palaces, built by the Minoans; the people are preparing for what will be known as the Trojan War. Tyre and Sidon are flourishing in what we now know as Iran, and the Elamites are at their very zenith in Mesopotamia. The code of Hammurabi is known, and in many ways it's enabling the Assyrians to expand their great world empire.

The Egyptians are constantly building; the famous King Tut may very well be at the height of his power. In Africa the Ethiopian dynasty is just beginning. In India you might see the very first signs of an Indian literature emerging. The potter's wheel, the calendar and brush writing are found in China. It is 2,500 years before Vasco da Gama, Magellan or Columbus. It is in the time of Joshua, the son of Nun.

As you get out of your time machine you will be standing on the edge of what historians and geographers like to call the Fertile Crescent. And there, the continuing drama of Hebrew history is being played out.

Although some things seem dramatically and drastically different to you, some things might be rather recognizable. For example, at about this time you will discover a highly secular period in the history of God's people. As we will see in our study of the book of Joshua, this is a very low point in terms of obedience to the revealed will of God. But if that is so, and it is, it is also a high point in the faithfulness and the promises of God. It is a time of theocracy.

Joshua is known as one of the former prophets, and this particular section of the Bible is recognized as part of the historical books. Like the rest of Scripture, the book of Joshua sets forth the gospel of the grace of God. It does so in an entirely different way from that of the Gospel of John, however.

But in Joshua no less than in John, we see that God works out the salvation of man. In a body the hand does not have the same function as the eye, but both are members of a living body and work together, each with a separate and yet distinct responsibility. So it is with these books. Each part of Scripture contributes to our total biblical portrait of the Lord Jesus Christ.

Continuity in God's Work

Joshua has much to teach us about our Lord. First, note that there is continuity in God's work. The book of Joshua points this out in a very sharp and clear way. Four hundred years before this period, God promised a country to a man named Abraham. God said to him, "Leave your country, your people and your father's household and go to the land I will show you" (Gen. 12:1). But Abraham never possessed that land. In fact, when his beloved wife Sarah died, Abraham had to negotiate with local landowners in order to get a piece of land large enough to bury her (see Gen. 23).

Yet, 400 years later, as we pick up the thread of the story, God's promise to Abraham is about to be fulfilled. God does not neglect His promises. Christians today get uneasy because sometimes a few days go by, or maybe even a few weeks or months, and we don't see our prayers answered. We wonder if God has gone out of business, or if He is no longer going to be faithful to the promises He made.

There are perfectly good reasons for delays in the answering of prayers. For example, God said, "The sin of the Amorites has not yet reached its full measure" (Gen. 15:16). That was one of the basic reasons why Abraham was not able to have the land. When the iniquity of the Canaanites (of whom the Amorites were a part) was full and when they became impossible in terms of their immorality, they were driven out and the Israelites came in.

The book of Joshua also teaches us that God's plans are not dependent on man. We often think so. We wonder how God can ever work without using a specific person. But in a story such as this we see that God's plans are not dependent on particular people. Moses seemed absolutely irreplaceable; but he died, and the work of God did not stop. God put someone else in that position. "After the death of Moses . . . the Lord said to Joshua" (Josh. 1:1). God had already put His hand upon Joshua some 40 years

7

before Moses' death (see Exod. 17:8-13). God is constantly preparing His people for something He wants them to do.

The measure of God's work is not based on the strength or ability of individuals. God uses individual people, to be sure, and He uses the abilities that these gifted folks have. But God always has His Joshua ready when it is time for Moses to step aside.

A missionary serving in West Africa once wrote a letter to his home church telling of 10 people who were baptized in his village at Christmastime. He said that when the gospel first came to that village some 30 years earlier, the chief religious leader of the village vowed openly that there would never be a Christian baptism in that town. Yet, the 10 baptisms mentioned in the letter were not the first. While that man was standing there 30 years earlier, saying, "We'll never see a Christian baptism in this town," God was already at work.

That which we do in the name of the Lord Jesus Christ is never wasted. All that is earnestly given to Him as an offering to be used for His glory, God uses in building His Church and His Kingdom. We often do not know who is the most useful in the successes of God. Moses is dead; Moses' servant takes over.

And I encourage you, my friend, to work where God has put you. Be faithful to the task that is yours at the moment. Do what is required of you now, and do it enthusiastically, with a sense of commitment to the Lord. Then, according to His own plan and in God's time, He will open the door to another place He wants you to fill.

And in the process of serving God, do not forget the labors of those who precede you. Joshua was something of a harvester. The groundwork was laid by Moses, but God was pleased to let Joshua come in to be used after Moses' death.

When the Lord calls a man, He qualifies him to do the job He gives to him. Here a soldier was needed and Joshua was called. At Pentecost, Peter was chosen. When God wanted a man to blaze a trail in Asia Minor and across Southern Europe He picked Paul. God is forming, He is choosing, He is influencing, for His work will continue. Joshua is Exhibit A of that.

Joshua's Commission

Next, notice that there is a commission here that is peculiar to Joshua. God gives him that commission. God led the people right up to the verge of the River Jordan, but they have not yet crossed it. All the Promised Land is out there, on the other side of the river. God now gives His servant Joshua the responsibility of taking the people into the land.

The first nine verses of the book of Joshua seem to throb with the promises that God makes to Joshua. God says, "Look, I was with Moses, I'll be with you; as I have blessed Moses, I'm going to bless you. My work will continue. You be faithful; you do what I called you to do; you stick with the task that is yours for the moment and this task will be accomplished, and you'll be blessed of God." And that is Joshua's commission.

Have you heard God speak? Has God commissioned you? Perhaps you have not experienced anything quite so dramatic or overwhelming as Joshua did, but it is just as important for you to be available to the Lord. I believe that if our ears are attuned to God, if we're waiting with expectancy, if we're walking in the right kind of relationship with the Lord, we may expect Him to speak and to guide us in ways that we'll understand.

Joshua was previously commissioned by Moses to be a representative among the people (see Num. 27:18-23). Moses reassured Joshua that he was God's man (see Deut. 3:28). But after Moses' death Joshua had a first-person experience—God spoke to Joshua directly. I believe God will do that for us, but basically He does it through Scripture. I believe you may expect God to speak to you through His Word.

When my brother and I were young boys, our parents felt moved of God to leave their secular work and go into conference work. They came into contact with a group of Christian people who operated a conference ground. Anybody who applied to join their staff was asked, "What is your Scripture verse? What has God said to you that you can point to?" The elderly gentleman who ran that place learned some lessons in his earlier years, and all of those lessons centered on the fact that a believer had better be certain he is doing what God wants him to do. When things get tough, it's marvelous to be able to say to the devil, "This is what God wants me to do; I have sensed it through His Word."

Has God spoken to you? Before you make a move, before you determine that you will go in a certain direction, you should leave yourself open to the possibility that God is going to speak to you through Scripture in a very clear way. Are you open to what God may be saying to you through Scripture?

We are urged in Scripture to test and to try the spirits. We are warned of the counterfeit. We need to be sure God is leading us, and I think our assurance lies in the Bible. The Word of the Lord came to Joshua. Has the Word of the Lord come to you recently?

God told Joshua to cross over the Jordan, to be strong and to cause the people to divide the land. He said, "I will give you every place where you set your foot" (Josh. 1:3). The people had to occupy the territory, and it seems to me that they would be limited only by their unbelief and by their fears.

Claim to Spiritual Blessings

You see, we must claim the spiritual blessings God has made available to us. The letter to the Ephesians tells us that God has blessed us with all spiritual blessings in heavenly places in Christ (see Eph. 1:3). It seems to me that there are things to be won. I am careful here not to suggest that we earn our salvation; but there are prizes we can win through responsible, obedient Christian living. These lofty heights that God has made available to us are vantage points for activity and work. "We know that we have come to know him if we obey his commands" (1 John 2:3).

Freedom from Fear

The Bible talks a lot about freedom from the burden and bondage of sin. In Joshua we can see how God in His mercy and in His marvelous provision sets man free from fear, for fear can be conquered.

God sets us free from fear—but not always from difficulties or from problems. When our Lord said, "Do not let your hearts be troubled" (John 14:1), it was a recognition that trouble does abound. It is true for you and me. We are not set free from problems, nor does Scripture say that we are ever to be set free from difficulties; but the Bible does say that the believer in Christ may be set free from fear.

God spoke to Joshua in these majestic words: "Be

11

strong and courageous. Do not be terrified" (Josh. 1:9). As you come back to them again and again, you will receive the kind of encouragement and strength that Joshua received as you recognize these words as promises for you.

Joshua faced the most massive kind of uncertainty. All of us can identify with and feel for Joshua at this point. Moses was dead. Joshua had served Moses faithfully and effectively for many years. Most scholars agree that Joshua was almost 80 years of age when we pick him up here in this chapter. Here was a man who was not in the early days of his life, yet he was ready to prove himself, to test his mettle. He had faithfully served God in a kind of secondary capacity, so far as the world was concerned. But God used him, trained and prepared him for the task that now was his. The fact that God gave him a pep talk seems to indicate that Joshua was afraid.

Possess Our Possessions

We, too, can claim the promise of God's help, if we meet certain conditions. The first condition is that we must possess our possessions. I've borrowed that expression from the Bible. It comes from the seventeenth verse of Obadiah, which talks about the house of Jacob possessing its possessions. It seems to me this is something of what God is saying to Joshua and to you and me. God expects us to move forward and advance in spiritual growth and understanding.

We often do not go far enough in appropriating what God makes available for us. We do not appropriate the promises of God; we do not appropriate the provisions that God makes for His people. There is indeed an inheritance; not only the inheritance that God was talking about here for His chosen people that related to a land, but an inheritance that Paul talks about in the book of Colossians (see Col. 3:24).

Even as the children of Israel found resistance in receiving the inheritance that God promised them, so will you. You will be resisted in appropriating the inheritance that rightfully belongs to you as a believer.

The devil hates to see Christians enjoy their faith. It is one thing to worry about your faith and to fuss and sometimes fight about it, but it is quite another to enjoy it. And that is the one thing the devil will resist again and again if he can. He does not want you to glory in the Lord. You will be resisted as you try to appropriate that characteristic for your Christian life. The devil will remind you of many, many reasons why you have no business rejoicing in Christ.

If you are thankful for the grace of God that has given you forgiveness, the devil will try to point out some reason why that is not genuine. He'll try to keep you from walking with a spring in your step and a song on your lips; he will try to undercut your hopes for the future, your peace in this experience that God calls life. These things are your rights as a believer; they are part of the inheritance of the saints. But the devil will attempt to deprive you of these experiences.

Scripture says that the child of God is to put to death the lusts of the flesh, resist the devil and walk in obedience. What a joy it is to be liberated and set free from fear that keeps us from enjoying what God has provided for us. We will be resisted as we possess our possessions.

We need not expect to possess our possessions all at once. When God was giving instructions and making promises regarding the conquest of the land, He said to Joshua,

13

"I will not drive them out from before you in one year, lest the land become desolate and the wild beasts multiply against you. Little by little I will drive them out from before you, until you are increased and possess the land" (Exod. 23:29,30, *RSV*). It was not in the best interests of the people that they should march through the land in one fell swoop and be the conquerors overnight. It takes time and preparation to be what God wants us to be.

I can remember as a young man, just starting out in the ministry, I was so intent and so earnest, so desirous of being what God wanted me to be. I used to have visions of grandeur, I'm sure; I used to say, "Lord, I'll do anything you want me to do; I'll pay any price you want me to pay; just let me preach with power and with effectiveness. And let thousands of people come into the Kingdom of God." And then I could not understand why that did not happen, because I had prayed and had told God I would pay the price.

A lot of things have happened over the years since that time. I still pray that prayer every day and it is still a hope and a dream and something for which I will trust God until I die. But now I've learned that God sees that it is necessary to have some seasoning and some maturing, some growing. If I had only read that verse back in Exodus maybe it would have helped me a bit. "Little by little" (Exod. 23:30).

God says to you and to me, "Be faithful where you are, take care of the responsibility I have given you, take care of what I have given you in my service now, and in due time I will open up another door for you." It is sometimes hard for us to learn, but it is little by little. Have you learned that?

To do this kind of work little by little does something

for me that I may or may not want to have done, or that I may or may not see as a necessity. It makes me dependent on God. It keeps me in a constant state of dependency. That is when God uses His people, when we are trusting Him every day.

With my human inclinations, I would prefer that the land be secured all at once. Why do we have to cross the River Jordan? Why do we have to walk around the walls of Jericho until they fall down? Why do we have to fight the Canaanites? Why do we have to go mile by mile and sometimes inch by inch? Why can't it all be ours right now?

If the land could be secured at once, think what that would mean. It would take away all the danger and all the possibilities of error. But God says, "Ah, but it will be little by little; that way you will keep dependent on me." God says to His people, "You are going to get that land, but you will not get it all the first year. It will come little by little."

And that teaches you and me to lean upon the Saviour. Then there is no room for self-reliance. Maybe that is why Isaiah says, "Therefore will the Lord wait, that he may be gracious unto you" (Isa. 30:18, *KJV*). There is the moving, growing dynamic to our faith. God will lead us through the land, little by little, until we are increased and inherit the land. Possess your possessions.

Rely on the Promises of God

The second condition is that we are to rely on the promises of God. In the words of 2 Chronicles 20:12, "O our God, . . . we have no power . . . do not know what to do, but our eyes are upon you." There it is—that is the secret of the Christian life, that is the joy God imparts to us, that is the way fear can be conquered. The battle is not ours but God's. He will show Himself strong in our behalf.

God had already promised the people a land: "He will give their kings into your hand . . . . No one will be able to stand up against you" (Deut. 7:24).

Moses had to face the monarch of the mightiest kingdom on earth, the Pharaoh, and none could stand before Moses, not the Pharaoh's magicians, not his wise men, none of them. So, the apostle could say in the New Testament, "If God is for us, who can be against us?" (Rom. 8:31).

Joshua, also faced with powerful enemies, is given the same assurance: "As I was with Moses," said God, "so I will be with you" (Josh. 1:5).

We are encouraged by that wonderful promise in 2 Peter 1:4, "Through these he has given us his very great and precious promises, so that through them you may participate in the divine nature." We may confidently say with Jonathan, "Come, let's go . . . . Perhaps the Lord will act in our behalf. Nothing can hinder the Lord from saving, whether by many or by few" (1 Sam. 14:6). We may confidently say with Jehoshaphat, "O Lord, God of our fathers, are you not the God who is in heaven? You rule over all the kingdoms of the nations. Power and might are in your hand, and no one can withstand you" (2 Chron. 20:6).

Obey His Pattern

Finally, we must obey His pattern. Abraham had to break with the old life; he was called upon to act in unquestioning obedience to the revealed will of God.

The call from God always makes very definite demands on His people. We need to ask God to give to us scriptural understanding of the full implications of belonging to God through Jesus Christ and the responsibilities that are ours as believers. By faith, Scripture says, Abraham obeyed. Jesus became "the source of eternal salvation for all who obey him" (Heb. 5:9).

God said to Joshua, "Be strong and very courageous . . . that you may be successful wherever you go (Josh. 1:7). In verse 8, God says, "Do not let this Book of the Law depart from your mouth; meditate on it day and night, so that you may be careful to *do*." This is obedience.

God said, "Go in and possess your possessions." He said, "These promises are yours." But He also said, "You must obey."

One of the great illustrations of this principle is found in 1 Samuel 15. Samuel came before Saul and said, "You haven't done what God told you to do." Saul began to excuse himself; he said, "The people told me this," and, "The people told me that." Samuel said to Saul, "To obey is better than sacrifice, and to heed is better than the fat of rams" (1 Sam. 15:22). There is nothing that takes the place of obedience—quick, full, wholehearted obedience—on the part of the people of God. When we possess our possessions, rely on God's promises and obey God, fear is conquered.

Promises Require Obedience

God blessed Moses with remarkable power and accompanied Moses with remarkable ability. Now that same God promises to enable this man Joshua who was chosen to take Moses' place. But we must remember it is God's power, it is God's purpose that is in focus here. The vessel God uses—be it Joshua or anyone else—is of secondary importance.

In the New Testament the apostle Paul said, "I planted the seed, Apollos watered it, but God made it grow. So neither he who plants nor he who waters is anything, but

17

only God, who makes things grow" (1 Cor. 3:6,7). Here is the key to effective and meaningful service for the Lord: We are instruments to be used in God's service, as was Paul, as was Joshua, but the focus is upon God. Joshua became the tool, or the instrument, by which God fulfilled the purposes He had in mind.

Joshua has all of those promises—this first chapter is simply packed with promises—but he must rely on those promises and he must be faithful to the One who gave the promises. Promises require obedience.

Spiritual Preparation

In requiring obedience from His people, God does not neglect the spiritual preparation they need. In this preparation God's Word plays an important part. In the midst of His promises to Joshua, God included an exhortation to make the Word an important part of his life. "Be strong and very courageous. Be careful to obey all the law my servant Moses gave you; do not turn from it to the right or to the left, that you may be successful wherever you go. Do not let this Book of the Law depart from your mouth; meditate on it day and night, so that you may be careful to do everything written in it. Then you will be prosperous and successful" (Josh. 1:7,8).

In this passage we see the establishment of God's *written* word. It is interesting that Joshua is now to be guided by a written Word—"this Book of the Law." That was not the complete Bible as we know it today but it was the beginnings of it. And it was that which God Himself blessed and gave by way of instruction to His people. Joshua for the first time is instructed, as a leader of the people of God, to be responsible to written law. Abraham and Moses had obeyed the spoken Word of God, but now

Joshua is instructed to follow the written Word.

God's Word was to be supreme in the life of Joshua. It was above Joshua and he was to rule by it. All of Joshua's actions were to be regulated by this book of the law. The book contained more than good advice or counsel; it was a law that was binding upon the people. Thus this law had divine authority resting upon it. It was a rule with a capital *R*, a rule to walk and live by.

In our day there are many who question the authority of God's Word, and many who simply ignore it. Yet even those who question or ignore God's revelation are seeking some meaning for life. Men have always agonized over the meaning of life. They have searched for God, as we can see in Acts 17; Paul came to Athens and said, "Men of Athens! I see that in every way you are very religious . . . I even found an altar with this inscription: TO AN UNKNOWN GOD" (Acts 17:22,23).

The human predicament is this: if a person has no faith in an authoritative Bible, where does he turn? He asks, "What is truth? What shall I believe?" Skepticism is the result when the authority of divine revelation is over-looked.

Some people, however, *are* listening for an authoritative voice, an answer. They are seeking answers today—any answer in some instances—and I believe our responsibility as Christians is to point these people to Scripture, for Scripture speaks with authority on the issues of life and death.

Joshua was charged to obey the Word because it was God's Word. That same charge is yours and mine. When men and women obey the Word, God blesses them. When they disobey, they bring trouble to themselves and others. Solomon heeded the evil that was in his heart and rejected

Scripture, and thus the decline in the nation began. Josiah was used by God to locate Scripture in the house of the Lord. He stood up and read it and the people were revived. Ezra did the same. Every time the people of God brought out the Word of God and read it and discussed it and decided that this is what God expected of them, God's blessing came down upon them.

"Do not let this Book of the Law depart from your mouth." The Bible is our guide, our rule of faith and practice. Notice that God also said to Joshua, "Meditate on it day and night." This means more than simply a passing glance at it. This means more than just listening to it being preached.

Christians need a disciplined study of Scripture. When we find ourselves moving ahead, grasping new truth, it is because we are meditating upon the Word of God. Paul said, "If anything is excellent or praiseworthy—think about such things" (Phil. 4:8). That means meditating on the Word of God.

I do not know any way you can do that except to take time, to purposely and in a disciplined way set aside time. You need to work on this in order to have the influence of God's Word in your life, to offset the things of the world. The world is full of influences that run counter to godliness, that tend to draw us away from the spiritual implications of the Word of God. Even the necessary activities of life—job, school, work at home—can crowd out spirituality.

God said to Joshua, "Here is the law; you are to abide by it. Here are the rules and regulations by which I expect you to live; here is the guidance I have made available for you. But you must meditate upon it so that you can obey it in its fullness."

Are the Scriptures speaking to you? If not, get into a Sunday School class, get into a Bible class. Know what it is to meet with some fellow Christians and study the Word of God. Go over the Word often. Let Scripture speak to your heart, day and night.

Temporal Preparation

Spiritual preparation was important to Joshua and the people of Israel. But temporal preparations were necessary too. Joshua told the people, "Get your supplies ready. Three days from now you will cross the Jordan" (Josh. 1:10). This had not been their custom; for years they received manna from heaven. In Joshua 5 the manna ceases; but here in chapter 1 Joshua is already instructing the people to begin to do things differently.

God provided the kind of help the people needed for life in the desert. There in that wilderness experience, the labor of the Israelites could produce nothing. But here, in a new set of circumstances, their own labor could do something. God's gifts to His people are appropriate. He will help us do what we have to do, but He will probably not do it for us.

And so Joshua says to the people, "Get ready, there are some things you can do to prepare for this experience of crossing the River Jordan."

What is God asking you to do in the preparation of your own life today? It costs something to possess the land. Out of the wilderness experience you have had, out of the rivers you have crossed, out of the enemies you have faced, there comes a stream of blessing and experience you can get no other way. There are some things that can come to the people of God only through difficulty and trial. Now that is not saying you are to go out and look for trou-

21

ble, but there are some things you will never learn in your walk with God except through trial and the discipline of difficulty. It costs something to possess the land.

We need to recognize the desert lessons that are ours. The book of Joshua has some of the most marvelous promises of any book in the Old Testament; but they come out of the context of crossing the Jordan River, of Canaanite enemies to conquer and of wilderness journeys. The same thing will be true for you.

Disposition of the Land

Finally, notice the disposition of the land. God, through Joshua, says that two-and-a-half tribes—Reuben, Gad and half the tribe of Manasseh—are to have the land on the east side of the Jordan. Now remember, the children of Israel are poised at the Jordan River; they are about to cross over and face all the enemies encamped in the land. And all of a sudden God says to Joshua, "Two-and-a-half tribes of you stay here!" How strange. The whole army of Israel fought against the enemy on the east side of Jordan—all of them, not just the two-and-a-half tribes we read about here. Yet now God gives the land to only a portion of those who did the fighting. This looks like an inequality, until you remember it was all arranged beforehand (see Num. 32). But learn this: God has His own ways and reasons for disposing of His gifts.

Some people are better-looking than others. Some are better students than others because of innate ability. Some are better teachers than others. These differences are part of the facts of life. What do we do about it? Do we resent it? Do we fight against it? Do we say, this is not fair?

Some people have to struggle with problems other

22

people do not have to struggle with at all. The Bible says, "Do not let the sun go down while you are still angry" (Eph. 4:26). Some people who do not have any temper look at that verse and say, "That's nothing—I don't let the sun go down while I'm angry because I don't get mad." But the fellow who is beset by a temper that has hounded him for years, whose fuse is very short, has to struggle again and again to let the grace of God operate in his heart to overcome his temper. We all have different kinds of temptations, we have different kinds of weaknesses and strengths. We have in that sense an inequality.

Some farmers get rich; some get washed away in a flood. Some people are never sick; some people seem to be sick all the time. Some good people seem to suffer everything, and some not-so-good people seem to prosper.

We are not omniscient, so we cannot explain the variables of human life. Look at the earth. We could ask ourselves why it is not one vast plain, or all pleasant hills, or all majestic valleys. Why is there an Iceland? Why is there a Sahara Desert? Why is not life one perpetual summer or springtime? Scripture says it is as it is because this is God's plan.

Scripture says we are to bear one another's burdens (see Gal. 6:2). These two-and-a-half tribes had it made. But they were assigned responsibility to help others, and so are we. There is an equality in all of this.

There is an interesting story in 1 Samuel. During a battle with the Amalekites, some of David's troops went into battle. But 200 soldiers, who were too near collapse to fight, stayed with the equipment. When the battle was won, some of the fighters suggested that the nonfighters should not share in the spoils. But David said they should all have equal shares (see 1 Sam. 30). God's people should share with one another. We are all members of the same body, the same family. God has given of this grace freely to us, so we should freely share with our brothers and sisters.

2
Mission
on My Mind

Joshua 2

As part of the preparation for entering the land, two members of what we might call the Hebrew Central Intelligence Agency received orders from their commander-in-chief, Joshua. They were told to leave the area of Shittim (which got its name from the abundance of acacia trees growing there) and to go to the city of Jericho. They had to hike about five miles before they came to the Jordan River, and another five or six miles from there to Jericho.

Once in Jericho, the spies were guided by God to Rahab's house. The account tells us that the king of Jericho had his own intelligence system, so he heard at once of the arrival of two Israelites. That's not surprising, for all of the area—Jericho and the surrounding countryside—surely must have been aware of this strange army of people. For 40 years these people lived in the desert south of Jericho. In fact, Rahab's comment was, "I know that the Lord has given this land to you and that a

25

great fear of you has fallen on us . . . . We have heard how the Lord dried up the water of the Red Sea for you when you came out of Egypt" (Josh. 2:9,10).

The king even knew that Rahab had taken in the spies. So he sent his men to Rahab's house to demand the men. Rahab lied and the posse that was after the Hebrew people was diverted to the desert to search for the two men.

Then Rahab, who was the owner of the house, elicited a promise from the spies to spare her family when the invasion came. (Note that she knew it was coming.) The two men agreed. They suggested that a scarlet cord (or rope) hanging in the window would be the identifying mark and would provide salvation for her household.

Rahab let the two men through a window and down over the wall by means of a rope. They fled to the nearby mountains, then slipped back across the Jordan River and reported their findings.

Interestingly enough, 38 years before, Joshua himself was sent by Moses to spy out the land. And he reported back to Moses that victory was theirs, just as these men now were telling Joshua. "The Lord has surely given the whole land into our hands; all the people are melting in fear because of us" (Josh. 2:24).

Promises and Personal Responsibility

We see in this story a basic truth—*the promises of God do not free us from work*. How far are precautions and efforts to be coupled with the promised help of God? I think Scripture indicates a balance. As we look again at the first few verses of Joshua 2, it seems that Joshua has a problem. He has to discern between idle trust and active cooperation. Remember, Joshua had been promised the land. Chapter 1 makes that very clear. Yet the moment we close chapter 1, with its marvelous abundance of the promises of God, we open chapter 2 to find Joshua sending out spies as if success depended on his organization, leadership and planning. Not so. Joshua sends out spies to find out what his people are up against.

The battle that is forthcoming is the Lord's. God has already said so; He will say it again. The people know this is true—the battle is the Lord's. So the spies' information really will not influence the outcome. God has already worked that out.

But God never intended that His help should make us idle. Proverbs 3:5,6 tells us to "trust in the Lord with all your heart and lean not on your own understanding; in all your ways acknowledge him, and he will make your paths straight." This is a truth many of us depend upon again and again, and rightfully so. But there is a word of warning for there is a danger that we might misuse this promise of God. God's promise to direct our paths was not given to us so that we could be irresponsible and His assurances are not meant to make us idle.

Joshua chapter 1 is full of marvelous promises. But these promises, as we have seen in chapter 2, are to be seen and experienced in the light of personal responsibility. There is work to be done.

When we belong to God and receive His promises, we are also charged with being responsible believers. We walk in the light of the promises of God, promises that say "I will be with you—don't be afraid." But we *work* in the light of God's promises as well. This has nothing to do with our salvation; we cannot work for our salvation. But we are not to trust God to do what He expects us to do.

God expects you to do your school work. He expects you to be a good preparer in terms of your preaching. He

27

expects you to be the best doctor—or anything else—God has called you to be. After we have done all that we can do, then it is in the Lord's hands.

A preacher of another generation had an extremely difficult week. Pressure was on him from all angles. Suddenly it was Sunday, and he was not well prepared. As he got ready to go up into the pulpit, he asked the Lord to help him, "Lord, you know I've had a busy week. I'm not really ready for this sermon today, so please help me."

And his own testimony was this: A word came to him as clearly as can be; a voice said, "Have you done your best in getting ready for this sermon?" And upon reflection he felt he could honestly say, "Yes, I've done the best I could do." And immediately, according to his testimony, the voice came back to him and said, "Then I will bless your efforts. If you have done the best you can do, I'll take over from here."

We have the responsibility to do the very best we can. We cannot expect God to answer prayers until we have done all we can do. We should not get so involved in working for God and doing so many different things for Him that we neglect our duty. Then, at the last minute, we come to the Lord and say, "Now Lord, you know I've been very busy in your work this week and I really do not have this other thing ready, so it's up to you."

That is presuming on God. I believe God asks us to fulfill our responsibilities to the very best of our abilities. And then, if there are lacks, He will make up for them. We are to fight the good fight of faith.

God told Joshua, "I will not fail you." Joshua responded by telling his spies, "Go view the land." Herein is a good balance. Work, as well as believe. Cromwell said, "Trust God and keep your powder dry," a balance. God expects us to do what we can do. The promises of God do not relieve us of the responsibility of work.

Priority of Choice

Sometimes in our relationship to God we have to make choices. Rahab chose to help the spies and in doing so she lied. But how are we to view that lie? Certainly we would say the end does not justify the means. I think it is true that a lie is never really pleasing to God. In Rahab's situation, we must look deeper into the Scriptures for certain principles.

Paul, in Romans 13:1, tells us: "Let every soul be subject unto the higher powers" *(KJV)*. We are to submit to human government, to obey the law, to pay our taxes. Jesus said, "Give to Caesar what is Caesar's, and to God what is God's" (Luke 20:25). But sometimes we must qualify these commandments in this way: When the authorities require of us anything that is obviously contrary to God's will, our first duty is to God.

Remember the three Hebrews who were cast into the furnace because they refused to worship the king's image? (See Dan. 3:8-30.) Remember Daniel, cast into the den of lions because he prayed even when he was forbidden to pray? (See Dan. 6:1-24.) Remember the apostles who said, "We must obey God rather than men" (Acts 5:29)? Peter, in his epistle, gives us good advice along this line. He says, "Fear God, honor the king" (1 Pet. 2:17). We are to obey the government cheerfully when it is consistent with our fearing God.

Note that Rahab had to choose between God and her country. I believe we owe fidelity to the place where we live. In America we are especially blessed. But we need discernment to see the things about our system we should

29

not accept. We must trust God to keep our priorities straight. This is not God versus country, but it is having God enlighten us in terms of biblical perspective so that we know how to put first things first. This was something of a problem for Rahab. She said to these men, "I know you're coming in. I know you're going to destroy this country. We are all aware of that. I'm asking that you keep us in mind as a family when you do."

People respond differently to God's presence. This whole country we are reading about in Joshua 2 knew about Israel. All of them had heard, all of them had trembled, but apparently only Rahab moved across the line into faith.

When the Saviour revealed Himself after the Resurrection, some believed. Why didn't everybody believe? In a way, from a human point of view, they all had the same chance. They all saw Him, but only some believed. When Paul preached in Athens, some believed and some did not. Jesus said, "He who has ears, let him hear" (Matt. 11:15). Priority of choice rests upon each one of us. All the people in Jericho had the same opportunity, but only Rahab said, "I ask for mercy." Many hear the gospel, yet all do not believe.

Place of Integrity

Finally, we should note the place of integrity. There is an emphasis upon oaths and promises in this chapter.

In verse 12 of Chapter 2, Rahab says, "Now then, please swear to me by the Lord." That is interesting; a woman, who a short time before blatantly lied, now says, "I want you to swear to me by God. I really want the truth from you."

The men gave Rahab the assurance of their word.

They said, in effect, "As representatives of the land of Israel, we give you our word and we make you this promise." So Rahab's safety and her family's safety depended upon whether or not these were men of integrity.

Integrity is essential. There is no substitute for it. We must have integrity in order to exist in our society today. We have to trust the people in the banks and the post office system, for example. We have to have a system that is undergirded by the morals of integrity.

We cannot survive in America without integrity in Washington. We cannot survive in our states without integrity in our capitals. A scrupulous use of the millions of tax dollars that are collected in this nation demands integrity. "Righteousness exalts a nation, but sin is a disgrace to any people" (Prov. 14:34).

Be a man or woman of integrity. You may be only one, but God needs people of integrity to hold back the tide of evil. Toynbee said that religions, with their definite value systems, are the elements holding the world's civilizations together. And a society that believes in nothing, that commits itself to nothing, that has no purpose or common goal, unravels and comes unglued.

Let us take our example from Joshua's spies and from the weight of testimony in God's Word; with God's help, let us be persons of integrity.

3
Miracles Among Us

Joshua 3

How do you handle your troubles? Do you curse them? Do you attempt to ignore them, to cover them up and hope somehow they might go away? Do you tell everyone your troubles? Most of us have troubles all right, and so most of us need to know what Scripture has to say about overcoming them.

The Jordan River is often pictured as an obstacle to overcome. Sometimes in songs and poems it is seen as that last cold barricade to cross over before reaching heaven, so it is referred to as death. But the Jordan River can illustrate for us a new kind of understanding of the Christian experience. Life on one side of that river is a desert filled with self-efforts and self-concern. Those who live on that side of the Jordan occupy themselves largely with personal efforts to accomplish things. In contrast, those who live on the other side of the Jordan exemplify the Christ-filled life—a life of faith and obedience.

Israel is poised now on the banks of the Jordan. Their 40 years of experience in the desert are behind them. They were wonderfully led of God and marvelously provided for by Him. Manna came down at night and rocks sometimes gave water. God took care of His people all through their wandering for those 40 years. Now, on the banks of the Jordan, the promises of God seem to fill the air. God says to them over and over again, "As I was with Moses, I will be with you; do not be afraid; launch out, press on; I will see that you accomplish my purpose."

The voice of Joshua can be heard as well, and Joshua speaks with authority and assurance. The people are delighted that God's hand is upon this man. God gave them strong and marvelous leadership in Moses; now that Moses is dead, Joshua is on the scene. Precious promises, glorious encouragement from God and His persistent claims upon these people; this is how we find the children of Israel on the banks of the Jordan.

Divine Presence

We can see throughout these 40 years of experience the divine presence of God. God was with Moses, but Moses did not always have that assurance. He started out pretty shaky, even fearful. He was so fearful that he objected to God, "Why would you call on me? I don't know how to lead these people; I don't have the necessary gifts or abilities." Even in the face of God's assurances and wonderful power, Moses was still fearful.

God had to give Moses two dramatic experiences to help convince him. One was the experience with Moses' rod. God said, "Take the rod that is in your hand and throw it on the ground." He did so and the rod became a serpent. Then God said, "Reach out your hand and take it by the tail." As Moses did so, it turned again into the rod. This must have been fantastically impressive to Moses.

The second experience was even more personal. God said, "Put your hand inside your cloak." Moses did that and when he drew his hand out it was leprous. Then God said to Moses, "Now put it back into your cloak." When he pulled it out this time, it was healed and cleansed. These final acts of God were necessary to convince Moses that God meant business. Thus assured, Moses went forth (see Exod. 4:1-9).

I am glad the Lord is so gracious that He will periodically give us the undergirding and support we need. We have His help in Scripture and we have it in the work of the Holy Spirit as He continues to minister and to open people's eyes to see and their hearts to believe. "When he putteth forth his own sheep, he goeth before them" (John 10:4, *KJV*). That is the assurance of His divine presence in our lives.

God's presence is guaranteed; and it seems to me that whenever we believe that guarantee and put our trust in God's promises, the very faith we are exercising comes under fire. We can interpret this as a time of testing. When we are greatly blessed of God, when there is spiritual advance and progress in our lives, then we should look out for some additional pressure to be applied against us for additional testing of that faith we have exercised.

There is another way to look at the pressures of life. They provide a great opportunity to exercise our trust in God's promises.

Which way do you interpret the situation in Joshua 3? As a test or an opportunity? I am inclined to think the latter may be a more positive lesson for us. Here are the people of God who have received promise after promise from Him. Things have gone wonderfully well for them; God's Spirit has been upon them in remarkable guidance and leadership. They have come through 40 years of desert wandering and now their goal is in sight. But between them and their goal stands the River Jordan, a huge and terrifying obstacle. How in the world does this great mass of people get across the Jordan River? Is the Jordan just a further obstacle to test their faith or is it a golden opportunity to exercise the trust that God said they should have in Him?

Perhaps we need to learn to look on problems not as obstacles but as opportunities. God gives us promises and experiences. We know that God is faithful (see Ps. 89:1); we know that no good thing will He withhold from the people who walk uprightly (see Ps. 84:11); we know that the steps of a good man are ordered by the Lord (see Ps. 37:23); we know that all things work together for good to the people that love God (see Rom. 8:28). In light of these promises perhaps we ought to look upon our obstacles as golden opportunities to exercise the trust God wants to elicit from us, His people. That is a more positive approach. When we have that attitude, then we can look upon our trials and unpleasant circumstances as occasions to prove the sufficiency of God. He never fails those who trust Him; He will never fail us as we commit ourselves to Him.

God's people in Joshua 3 face a great obstacle. They have come to the end of their own resources. For three days Joshua was getting them ready. But also during those three days they were looking at perhaps the most formidable obstacle they had ever faced in 40 years of wandering. The Jordan River is at flood level, according to Joshua 3:15. That means that it is very wide and swift. There are no boats, there is no bridge, and yet God said, through His servant Joshua, that the people are going to cross this obstacle and reach the other side. The people of God could be at peace, Joshua could continue to lead with authority and assurance, because God's divine presence was with them!

In the desert the pillar of cloud and fire were visible signs of God's leading and His people were not to move until the sign was evident. The presence of God with Joshua and the Israelites was symbolized by the Ark of the Covenant. The Ark was a covered box about 45 inches long and 27 inches wide and deep, made of acacia wood. There were golden rings on each corner into which gold-covered poles were inserted (see Exod. 25:10-15). By these poles the Ark was carried from place to place. Inside the Ark were kept the copies of the law God gave Moses, a portion of the manna from the desert and the rod of Aaron that budded. The Ark was associated with life and glory and direction. The very presence of God came to that box.

We see a similar leading of God in the New Testament. In Acts 1:4, Christ told His followers to stay in Jerusalem and wait for the promise of the Father. Earlier He told them, "Apart from me you can do nothing" (John 15:5). God's people in the New Testament were to do nothing until they saw the presence of God and knew that He was leading them. When the day of Pentecost came the people were given a manifestation of God's presence. "Suddenly a sound like the blowing of a violent wind came from heaven and filled the whole house where they were sitting. They saw what seemed to be tongues of fire that separated and came to rest on each of them" (Acts 2:2,3).

We see signs of God's divine presence again and again

in the Scriptures. He continues to be with His people today. Have you recognized God's hand in your life recently? Have you sensed His guidance in your activities and circumstances? God promises us He will never leave us nor forsake us, just as He promised the Israelites in the wilderness; just as He promised His followers in Jerusalem.

The manifestations of God have been different in different ages and at different times. It does not really pay for us to look back and say, "Why doesn't the Lord do it exactly the same way today that He did 100 years ago?" Maybe He will, but that really is not the significant thing. What we really want is the divine presence of God—and we should let Him work it out the way He wishes. What the people of God really wanted was God's presence. I would not think it mattered to them whether it was a cloud or a fire or a box or whatever, so long as God was manifesting His presence.

We need to seek God's guiding hand today. It is a joy to follow the Lord Jesus Christ. There is nothing so satisfying as being in the will of God. To follow the Lord Jesus Christ is not always easy. But knowing and following God's will is a joyful thing—the greatest thing in all the world. I hope you know His divine presence.

Divine Holiness

This chapter also speaks of divine holiness. In Joshua 3:4 we see that there is to be a space between the people and the Ark. I think God commanded that space be left between the Ark and the people so that *all* the people would be able to see the Ark. They needed to be assured of God's guidance and direction, for they had not "been this way before."

37

Usually we interpret verse 4 of Joshua 3 to refer to the route they were to travel. They had not been in this geographical area before. But there is another possibility. It might mean, "You have not traveled in this *manner* before." The cloud seems to be gone. The Ark is now the symbol of the Lord's presence. It is not only that they had not traveled this way before, it is also that they had not traveled *in this fashion*, the way in which God is providing for them.

Now Joshua calls upon the people to sanctify themselves (see v. 5). This is the same injunction Moses received in Exodus 19:10, when God told the people to clean themselves up, sanctify themselves and set themselves apart for the glory of God.

The New Testament, too, has a clear message of sanctification. "Let us purify ourselves from everything that contaminates body and spirit, perfecting holiness out of reverence for God" (2 Cor. 7:1). "If a man cleanses himself . . . he will be an instrument for noble purposes, made holy, useful to the Master and prepared to do any good work" (2 Tim. 2:21). "Everyone who has this hope in him purifies himself, just as he is pure" (1 John 3:3).

We long to see God at work in wonders and in power today. But sometimes God withholds His power. He wants clean vessels. God can never fill us as long as we are experimenting to see how far and how fast we can travel with the world. Power for the gospel follows upon cleansing. The Bible teaches us to shun that which defiles and to devote ourselves to God's service and let Him work through us. As the apostle Paul says, "Since you have taken off your old self with its practices and have put on the new self, which is being renewed in knowledge in the image of its Creator" (Col. 3:9,10). That is the kind of divine holiness that God expects to see in your life and in mine.

Divine Wonder

Finally, note the divine wonder that God provides (see v. 5). "Consecrate yourselves, for tomorrow the Lord will do amazing things among you." The Christian life is exciting. The question that confronts us each day is, "What is God going to do next?" Do not fear that problem with which you are confronted, do not fear that obstacle that rolls before you, that Jordan River. Face it with confidence, for God is capable of dealing with it. Said the people of God, "We have no power . . . we do not know what to do, but our eyes are upon you" (2 Chron. 20:12). That is a good reminder for us. Let us keep our eyes upon Him, for He has the power to do that which we cannot.

God's Provision for Crossing the Jordan

In the northern part of Italy there is a small river named the Rubicon. It flows for about 15 miles into the Adriatic Sea. Julius Caesar crossed that river in 49 B.C., and in the process of doing so he initiated a great civil war. Today the expression "to cross the Rubicon" means to commit oneself irrevocably in a certain direction.

The rivers of the world are important to humanity. They provide geographical boundaries, transportation, food and scenic beauty. School children learn of the great rivers of the world—the Mississippi, the Missouri, the Rhine, the Amazon.

But in the Bible, it is the Jordan—no hesitation, no question—it is the Jordan River. There are other rivers mentioned in the Bible, but Jordan is *the* river.

The Jordan's sources are the great slopes of Mount

Hermon. Between the Sea of Galilee and the Dead Sea, the Jordan flows through a deep depression known as the Ghor. The valley of the Ghor is three miles wide at the north and 12 miles wide at the city of Jericho. The riverbed itself, known as the Zar, is a quarter of a mile to two miles wide and runs 65 miles from the Sea of Galilee to the Dead Sea. The Jordan itself is a winding, snakelike river, and thus it covers many more than 65 miles in its meanderings.

Many important events in the Bible—including the baptism of our Lord Jesus—took place along the Jordan. Here in the book of Joshua, we come to one of these important events—Israel crossing the Jordan River.

Magnification of God's Man

Before the Israelites cross the Jordan, God does something most unusual. "The Lord said to Joshua, 'Today I will begin to exalt you in the eyes of all Israel'" (Josh. 3:7). This is a startling statement in any set of circumstances but particularly in the Bible. It would be less surprising if God said to Joshua, "Today, I'm going to begin to humble you; that's what you need."

The last thing most of us need is magnification. To magnify a man, to lift him into a place of honor, to put the spotlight of attention upon him so that people begin to think, "What a fine, outstanding leader he is" is a dangerous thing. And in Scripture, not very many people have been magnified. I think one of the reasons why God apparently gives so few people genuine honor, magnifies so few people, is that so few people can handle it. Magnification, like great sums of money, carries its own built-in danger. Honor, such as God is about to give Joshua, would be the ruination of most of us .

God warns us, "Pride goes before destruction, a haughty spirit before a fall" (Prov. 16:18). Honor is a dangerous thing. Scripture calls for humiliation, not for honor.

But God said, "Joshua, I'm going to exalt you." I wonder how Joshua reacted. I wonder if he asked for a special outpouring of God's mercy and grace. I wonder if he fell on his face in the dust and said, "Oh, God, do you know what you're doing with this frail vessel?" This must have been a startling, terrifying and overwhelming announcement from God.

But the fascinating thing is that Joshua goes to Israel and says nothing at all about his newly magnified position. Here is a very important lesson for us. Worldly honors may call forth a worldly spirit. The Christian spirit always wears honor with great humility. If we do not wear the garment properly, God may take it from us.

Of course, God is not petty and He is not jealous in the sense that you and I think of jealousy. But it does say in the Bible, "I, the Lord your God, am a jealous God" (Exod. 20:5). God will not share His glory with another. Paul said, "May I never boast except in the cross of our Lord Jesus Christ" (Gal. 6:14). God does not want us taking the glory and getting ourselves all puffed up with pride. But remember also that He is our loving heavenly Father, a merciful God who know our frailties.

We need to guard our attitudes, we need to be very cautious and very careful. Then God can use us and bless us and work out all that He wants to do in and through us. But if He has to work His way around us in terms of pride or a puffed-up spirit, His program and His purposes will slow down.

God said to Joshua, "Today I'm going to exalt you." It is marvelous and it is frightening. But God is marvelous in the way in which He takes care of us. If we walk very earnestly and softly before Him, and if we are very careful to give God the glory, then He is going to keep us from falling into that pride, that haughty spirit He despises. It is wonderful to see how God works these things out and keeps us humble.

Seek the lowly place, and let God be the one who says to you, "Come up higher." That was the teaching of our Lord in the parable. When you go to a dinner party, He said, seek the lower seats, don't seek those chief places. And if the host is of a mind to honor you, he'll ask you to come up (see Luke 14:10). That is a picture of our service for God. Walk quietly before the Lord. And if God should do for you what He did for Joshua, then double your prayer time and ask Him for the grace and the genuine Spirit-filled humility you will need.

Magnification of God's Word

Now notice what Joshua said to the children of Israel: "Come here and listen to the words of the Lord your God" (Josh. 3:9). Joshua turned the people to the words of God. There is no greater invitation in all the world than the invitation to come and hear the words of the Lord God. We need to recognize God's Word as God's Word, and we need to bring our lives into obedience to that Word.

There is a remarkable story in Jeremiah 36, an Old Testament description of the writing of a prophetic book. God gave Jeremiah a message that Babylon was going to invade and conquer the land of Israel. Jeremiah dictated the message to his secretary, Baruch, and since Jeremiah was not allowed in the Temple at this time, he sent Baruch to read the message to the people.

The princes heard of the message, so they sent for

42

Baruch to read it to them. When they heard of the coming invasion, they were most concerned. They knew the king must be told, but first they told Baruch and Jeremiah to hide.

The princes reported to King Jehoiakim, and he had a man named Jehudi read the message to him. As Jehudi read from the scroll, the king cut off sections of it with his knife and threw them into the fire that was burning in the room. Such contempt for God's Word and God's warning!

Joshua said to the people, "Come, don't ignore the Word of the Lord. Come and listen to it: come and see what God has for you." Revelation springs from the very nature of God. God makes Himself known. Because He is the God of redemption, He is also the God of revelation. In Christ, as we know from the New Testament, there is atonement for sin.

God has been reaching out to humanity from the beginning. Way back in the book of Genesis, God called to Adam in love, "Adam, where are you?" The whole Bible is the history of God's redemptive love. God has spoken, sometimes in storms and thunder, sometimes in a still, small voice. He has spoken through priest and prophet and sage and singer—and finally He spoke through the Lord Jesus Christ. So the story of revelation in the Bible is the story of progression to the person of the Lord Jesus Christ.

God's truth abides. We cannot suppress it. His truth shall indeed reign supreme—and because of that, we are to obey it and to be blessed by it.

Magnification of God's Provision

Notice the magnificent provision of God for His people. The people passed over the River Jordan on dry ground (see Josh. 3:17). This required the faithfulness of God and faith on the part of the people. Jordan always rolls between us and the land, but it is God's purpose that we cross over.

We all stand on the bank of some Jordan River, and the beautiful land is over there—but oh, the things that hold us back, our own weaknesses, our own temperament, our own human nature. Look to Him. "Let us fix our eyes on Jesus, the author and perfecter of our faith" (Heb. 12:2). Let Him provide a way for you to cross that difficulty. He is the Head; we are simply the members of His Body. In all things He is to have the preeminence (see Col. 1:18). The Bible tells us, "When he putteth forth his own sheep, he goeth before them" (John 10:4, *KJV*).

Go to the edge of that difficulty: go as far as you can, do your utmost duty and leave the impossible to God. He has almighty power. He has infinite wisdom. Nothing is too hard for Him. He can do anything that He pleases. He controls the storm; He opens the seas; He makes the flinty rocks pour out fountains of water; He makes the ravens feed His servant Elijah. "If God is for us, who can be against us?" (Rom. 8:31). He will make your Jordan passable.

Remember this promise: "I have called you by name; you are mine. When you pass through the waters, I will be with you; and when you pass through the rivers, they will not sweep over you. When you walk through the fire, you will not be burned; the flames will not set you ablaze. For I am the Lord, your God, the Holy One of Israel, your Savior" (Isa. 43:1-3).

Here is God's provision for you, whatever your Jordan experience may be. Come to it in faith, in confidence. Trust God, and cross the Jordan.

4
I Remember, Lord

Joshua 4

Anthropologists are always digging up artifacts that have religious significance. They unearth the remnants of a temple that was used for worship. Or they come across small statues or an altar, and determine that the altar was used for some kind of sacrifice in relationship to the religion of that particular culture and time.

Once on the island of Ponope in the Central Pacific, I was taken in a small canoe up a shallow river until the river became just a bit of a creek. Then we got out and walked to a clearing in the jungle, and there were the most massive stone remnants I had ever seen, tucked away in the middle of nowhere. There were huge stone beams, carefully carved, some of them 40 feet long. Nobody knows exactly when they were made. The people who studied them consider them to to be some kind of relics of religious significance at least a thousand years old. Here is where people worshiped, offered sacrifices or gathered together in the name of their religion.

Have you ever thought what the archeologists of the future are going to find when they come to your city? When they uncover great structural remnants, piles of concrete and steel and brick, will they be able to discover what the churches really were?

Over in the Holy Land, in the city of Jerusalem, people like to say, "I walked today where Jesus walked." But the truth of the matter is that there's at least 10 feet of rubble piled on top of the original areas where our Lord walked. To go through all of that, to sift through the various cultures, is a fascinating and highly rewarding experience to the people who spend their time digging.

When we turn to Joshua chapter 4, we see that Joshua piled up stones as a memorial of the crossing of the Jordan. The stones would be a memorial for the children of Israel forever. As they crossed over the riverbed, miraculously made dry by God, they picked up 12 stones, one for each tribe. (Joshua also set up another 12 stones right in the riverbed.) When they got to Gilgal, they placed the 12 stones there as a monument.

A Word of Warning

Back in the third chapter, verses 9 and 10, Joshua said, "Come here and listen to the words of the Lord your God. This is how you will know that the living God is among you, and that he will certainly drive out before you" those various tribes.

There is a warning here for us: God is a living God, and thus He is not to be considered an idol in any form. Perhaps that doesn't mean as much to us as it did to the people a long time ago. But it does seem that the human mind has a craving for visible forms to express our conceptions. The problem of idolatry springs at us from page after page

46

of the Bible. The teraphim, for example, were the household gods of people; they carried them when they moved around from place to place. They depended upon them. They used them in what we would call wizardry or divination.

Idolatry seems to spring from a psychological source within us. The need for idols is not imposed externally, but seems to come from within. Idol worship has always been forbidden in the Bible.

The second commandment God gave to Moses talks about graven images. I do not think that it is necessarily a prohibition against artists and sculptors so much as it is a prohibition of idolatry. The Bible is full of warnings against idolatry. Over and over again Israel was tempted to succumb to the worship of idols. Ashtoreth, Chemosh and Moloch were all gods of pagan peoples around Israel, and Israel often adopted the worship of these various idols.

There are warnings in the New Testament, too, about idolatry. Idolatry in the New Testament is manifest by the works of the flesh. Covetousness, is idolatry (see Col. 3:5). Paul said, "Formerly, when you did not know God, you were slaves to those who by nature are not gods" (Gal. 4:8). These were idols.

God forbids idolatry, but I do not think there is a prohibition against symbolic reminders. For some people, symbolism is often very useful and can be most meaningful. Even here, in the fourth chapter of Joshua, it was quite in order that they should pile up those stones. And those stones became a monument, a reminder to the people who were to come after this generation of what God had done.

Nevertheless, God's people must be careful how they handle their reminders. God instructed Moses to erect a serpent of brass. That serpent was preserved by the peo-

47

ple of Israel for at least 600 years. Then Hezekiah, the good king who wanted to do what God was instructing him to do, had to destroy the serpent to stop the people of God from burning incense to it and worshiping it (see 2 Kings 18:4). Worship was never its intent. It was a symbol, a reminder, a way God worked out His mercy and His providence toward His people. But as time went by, the very thing God used to turn attention to Himself was worshiped.

The greatest thing in all the world is to realize that the living God is in your midst. That is what Joshua reminds the people in chapter 3, verse 10. As a warning, he says, "This living God, unlike those that are carved out of stone or wood, unlike those that may be represented by the bodies in the heavens, this living God is in your midst; and He sees, He hears, He knows, He's a living being." It is a warning against idolatry.

A Word of Encouragement

Joshua's statement about the living God is not only a word of warning, but also a word of encouragement. This God who is with us is faithful. He is faithful because of who He is; He is faithful because indeed He is a living God.

More than 400 years before Joshua, God told His servant Abraham, "Abraham, get out of your father's house, from your father's country, into a land which I will show you; I will make of you a great nation; your seed shall be like the stars and like the sand in the sea" (see Gen. 12:1,2; 15:5; 22:17). God promised Abraham a whole country, yet Abraham never lived to possess that country; he even had to negotiate for a cemetery plot when Sarah died. But God does not neglect His promises, and even after this long period of time, He is going to fulfill His promise. Four hundred years after God said to Abraham, "I will give you the land," He is going to do exactly that.

God is faithful to do for us that which He has promised. Because He is the living God, we can trust Him. What we do for God is never wasted. We are to work on that which God has given us to do. Be faithful, even as God is faithful.

I believe God performed the miracle described in Joshua 3 and 4, the crossing of the Jordan River, to encourage His people. God shows His sovereignty in this crossing.

Can you trust God's timing as it relates to your future? This living God is among you. You belong to Him through faith in the Lord Jesus Christ. He promises never to go away and leave you to your own devices. He promises to guide and direct you. God is at work in your life; He is working out the arrangements so that they fit beautifully together in just the direction He wants you to go. If you are worrying or stewing or uneasy about your future, if you are wondering if God has forgotten that you are around, I assure you, the living God is with you. If you will just be faithful to that which God has given to you up to this point, He will lead you on. God will open the door for the next responsibility He wants for you. God has a future for you; God knows where you can best serve Him; God is at work. He wants to minister to you. He *is* faithful.

Joshua and the Israelites raised a monument to the faithfulness of God. No doubt your life is marked by some of those monuments. But you cannot stop with monuments. Joshua says in the tenth verse that the living God is among them. He is going to see that they get across the river and He is going to *drive out the enemy*. God will go all the way. He will not do only part of the work and then walk off and leave you. Scripture says that He who has begun a

49

good work in you will complete it (will perfect it) until the day of Jesus Christ (see Phil. 1:6).

The Old Testament is a record of God's promises to the patriarchs, to the kings, to the prophets, to Israel, to the lowly saints, to the whole world at large. "Not one word has failed of all the good promises He gave" (1 Kings 8:56).

God promised us eternal life; God promised us forgiveness of sin and power for daily living. He promised us the answer to our prayers and guidance for our activities; He promised that this world is the scene for His work; He promised never to leave us as we go into all the world. He promised to rule and overrule; He promised that He will come again. Is all of this too good to be true? No! These are the promises of God.

A Word of Command

Finally, the living God also brings to us a word of command and that command is to *obey*. Joshua 3:8 says, "Tell the priests who carry the ark of the covenant: 'When you reach the edge of the Jordan's waters, go and stand in the river.'" Joshua 4:9 says, "Joshua set up the twelve stones that had been in the middle of the Jordan at the spot where the priests who carried the ark of the covenant had stood." Here is the promise of God that elicits obedience from His people. They had to stand still in the Jordan River. What a test! What a trying time! The people of God were not only ordered to advance to the edge of the swollen and raging river, but they were to stand in it. It seemed so ridiculous, and yet that was the order of God.

We are to go to the limits of that which God has opened up for us and then we are to trust Him for the rest. God's promises do not free us from work. We are not to have idle trust but active cooperation with the will of God. Are the overflowing banks of the Jordan River about to swallow you up? Do you suppose that their overflowing banks mean some kind of an obstacle to God? Of course not! It is just as easy for divine omnipotence to divide and dry up that river in its raging, swollen condition, as it would be if it were a little creek or a brook. It is all the same to the Lord. Do not despair, my friend, when the banks of your life seem to overflow. Stand still in obedience and trust this living God. The Lord will show Himself strong in your behalf.

In one of his books, Dr. V. Raymond Edman, a former president of Wheaton College, tells a remarkable story. One day, while Dr. Edman was president of the college, a student asked for permission to see him. When he came in, this freshman sat down in front of Dr. Edman. He didn't say a word, but anxiety and trouble were written all over his face. He pushed a piece of paper across the desk, a bill from the school's office. The bill stated the amount of money this young man owed; if he didn't pay it, he was going to have to leave. Dr. Edman picked it up and talked with the young man for a moment; he said, "I see the bill says $29.75."

The young man said, "Yes. I've prayed about this for several days. I've used up every penny I could possibly get my hands on, and I still owe the school that much money."

Dr. Edman said to him, "Well, how much money do you have?"

The student looked him straight in the eye and said, "I have 75¢, and that's all."

Then Dr. Edman said, "Turn that piece of paper over, young man. Write on the back this equation: 75¢ is to

$29.75 as five loaves and two small fishes are to 5,000 people." The young man looked at the equation, laid his pencil down, put his head on Dr. Edman's desk and asked the Lord to help him be faithful to what he knew was His promise.

Dr. Edman said that every time the young man came back to the campus to visit, he would come through the door, with a smile on his face, and say, "Seventy-five cents is to $29.75 as five loaves and two small fishes are to 5,000 people."[1]

There will come times in your life when you are going to have to take God at His word and trust Him. But remember this: Jesus said, "Why do you call me, 'Lord, Lord,' and do not do what I say" (Luke 6:46). God expects obedience from you and me. He warned us that the man who heard His sayings and did not heed them was like a foolish man who built his house on the sand (see Matt. 7:26). True happiness is found in implicit and full obedience to the Saviour.

The living God is here. This is a word of warning. But it is also a word of encouragement; He is faithful to His promise. And finally, it is a *word of command!* Stand still in the Jordan and let God work out for you that which is well-pleasing in His sight, for He *will* do it. You can trust Him. Remember that.

Footnote

1. V.R. Edman, *Not Somehow, but Triumphantly* (Grand Rapids: Zondervan Publishing House, 1965), p. 18.

5
Battle Stations!

Joshua 5,6

Israel's enemies were frightened. When they heard what God was doing for His people—dividing the Jordan River, drying up its bed—they knew they were in trouble! Because sin reigned and controlled in Canaan, the people collapsed when they saw Israel. In a sense, God was preparing the way for His people to conquer the people of Canaan.

But before they went into battle, before they took Jericho, the Israelites had a respite. God gave His people a time of rest. I believe God gives His people such a time for a purpose. Usually when God gives you a time of rest, the purpose is to renew you. It is to let you regather your forces, make new plans, gain new insights. A time of rest helps you to gain new strength to do what God wants done.

The people of Israel are preparing to receive their possessions. They are standing on the edge of them. The whole land is going to open up before them in a short while. God is going to bare His arm once again in mighty power. But now there is an interval of preparation. It is an interval of spiritual renewal in the lives of His people.

Do you make the most of such times when God provides them for you? Delays in your plans and delays in your circumstances give God a chance to teach you what He wishes. And I think the proper Christian response to those delays is to say, "Lord, what are the lessons you want me to learn while I am in this situation?"

Alan Redpath says: "We are always in a fever to *do* something for God. We've forgotten that the first thing God wants is that we *be* something for Him."[1] We are always anxious to do, to go, to be involved. God may want us only to learn to *be*.

Gilgal, as it is described in chapter 5 of Joshua, is on the edge of the desert, beyond the Jordan, on the east border of the city of Jericho; it is a place of waiting and a place of learning. These are not always easy things to do, no matter where we are. Most of us would find it much easier to rush on to Jericho and watch those walls come tumbling down. That is where the action is. That is where the battlefront is. We want to get into the activity. But Gilgal is an important stop. God often puts a Gilgal in the life of the Christian.

The Place of Renewal

We can learn some things from Gilgal. The first one is this: here is the place of renewal, the covenant of God. Years before, God made a covenant with Abraham (or Abram, as he was known at that time). "The Word of the LORD came to Abram in a vision: 'Do not be afraid, Abram. I am your shield, your very great reward.'" (Gen. 15:1).

And Abram said, "I am not so sure about that." He began to argue with God and to ask for evidence.

And God reassured him. God said, "Look up at the heavens and count the stars—if indeed you can count them. So shall your offspring be" (Gen. 15:5). And Scripture says, "Abram believed the Lord, and he credited it to him as righteousness" (v. 6).

Then God gave Abram some additional assurances. "Know for certain that your descendants will be strangers in a country not their own, and they will be enslaved and mistreated four hundred years. But I will punish the nation they serve as slaves, and afterward they will come out with great possessions" (Gen. 15:13,14). Then the Lord described the boundaries of the land He was going to give him (see vv. 18-21).

Part of the covenant that God made with Abraham involved the identifying mark of circumcision (see Gen. 17:10). But the Israelites had not been practicing circumcision since leaving the land of Egypt. The reason for the lapse was that the nation had been under judgment. Now the nation was in place where it must once again begin to obey God. They needed to be identified as the people of God once again.

That is always our need, to be re-identified as the people of God. We need to pick up where we have fallen away, to be restored, to be brought back to the place of permanent relationship with God. We need a time and place for renewal.

The people of God learned in Elijah's time that they had to be restored to God. Elijah challenged the prophets of Baal to a great contest to determine who worshiped the true God, the children of Israel or the prophets of Baal. Whichever god answered by fire would be recognized as the true God. The prophets of Baal cut themselves, punished themselves and cried all day; they made all kinds of pleas to the false god Baal, but nothing happened. And then at the close of the day, Elijah had his chance. He began by rebuilding the altar of God, which had fallen down. Elijah did not call for a new religion. He did not even ask for a new revelation of God. He went back to where the people left God in the first place. He rebuilt the altar. Then he waited for the fire to come from heaven. And as soon as the altar of God was rebuilt, the fire of God came down (see 1 Kings 18:19-38).

There is a great truth for us in this incident in terms of our relationship with God. God established the plan; He expects us to fulfill it. The Spirit of God reveals to the people of God that which is contrary to the will of God; and our responsibility is to break from what is contrary and obey the revealed will of God.

After Joshua caused the people to restore their obedience to God in the matter of circumcision, they then could engage once more in the Passover celebration (see Josh. 5:10). They encamped in Gilgal and they kept the Passover in the evening of the fourteenth day of the month, in the plains of Jericho. It was a joyous restoration—the people of God were once again having fellowship with Him.

Much of the Christian life and its success depends upon obedience. That is a key word. We always forfeit our right to blessing when we disobey God. God will not fill a church with joy, or a home with satisfaction, or a life with meaning, when His people disobey Him and ignore the teaching of the Scriptures.

Renewal in relationship to God seems to bring new fellowship. The Israelites could now remember with appreciation all that God had done. Years later this Passover was

56

to give way to the Lord's Supper that we Christians cele-
brate. And someday that will be gone, too. We will then
feast upon Christ.

But here is the joy of their fellowship being restored.
That time of wandering under the disobedience of their
own hearts, and under the judgment of God, has now been
wonderfully put behind them. So much of the time we
spend wandering around in desert experiences when God
wants us in His fellowship.

God can make a feast for us anywhere. Notice that the
people kept this Passover in the plains of Jericho. What a
place to enjoy the feast of fellowship with God—in the
very face of the enemy! They celebrated it in the face of
some of the greatest difficulties they were ever going to
see and at the conclusion of a very trying and difficult time.
But because God was there, it was a feast.

God can provide the feast of fellowship for us anywhere, so long as we are in right fellowship with Him, so
long as we are in an obedient response to His call. Then it
does not matter what the circumstance is. God fed Elijah
by the brook Kerith during famine time (see 1 Kings 17:2-
6). He gave Daniel a kind of peace and protection in the
lions' den (see Dan. 6:22). He enabled Peter to be able to
sleep in prison (see Acts 12:6). Indeed, as we are
reminded in Psalm 23, He is able to prepare a table before
us in the presence of our enemies. On the plains of
Jericho, in the face of the enemy, the people enjoyed the
Passover fellowship with God.

The Place of Change
Another significant event happened at Gilgal; the
manna no longer fell from heaven (see Josh. 5:12). The
manna had been part of the people's lives for a long time.

57

God provided it for the desert experience. Suddenly it stopped.

Now, the people had complained about the manna in the past (see Num. 11:5,6), but they learned that God was faithful to supply what He told them He would. There is a lesson here for us; manna was the mark of a wilderness state. When the people were in the wilderness, manna was what they needed. Now they are in the land. That land is theirs by covenant. Eating the fruit of the land is the first step toward the possession of the land. Manna is no longer needed.

The manna was for a special purpose. The fruit of the land is the normal, productive, dependable feeding that should be ours as we go through life. It is not as spectacular as the manna falling from heaven. It is not as filled with spiritual thrill as the manna falling from heaven. But it is the way of God. And if I can interpret it this way, I think we should be willing to leave the simplicity, the basics, the ABCs, and go on to feast on the Lord Jesus Christ Himself.

Many Christians seem to be waiting for those special kinds of manna. We wait for God to do something spectacular and thrilling from a spiritual point of view. However, that is not where we get our growth and our sustenance. We are to rejoice in the special kinds of manna and certainly we ought to take advantage of those things when they come. But the basic day-to-day routine of growing that God expects His people to do comes from the "fruit of the land": getting into the Scripture, day-by-day disciplined prayer life, understanding and seeking God's purposes and will.

God knows our necessities, whatever they may be. He sent manna to feed the Israelites in the wilderness. He sent the ravens to feed Elijah during a famine. But God inspired Paul to write: "Work with your hands" (1 Thess. 4:11). Also, when Peter was in prison, God sent an angel to strike down chains from which Peter could not free himself, chains which were holding him and preventing him from getting out. But the angel did not pick Peter up and carry him. Rather, the angel said to Peter, "Put on your clothes and sandals. Wrap your cloak around you and follow me" (Acts 12:8).

God is as almighty and as powerful today as He was in the days of Joshua. But God expects us to feed off the fruit of the land and use the provisions that He puts before us so that we may grow and develop. He will not do for us what we can do for ourselves.

The Place of God's Appearance

The last few verses of chapter 5 describe another incident that happened at Gilgal: Joshua's encounter with the captain of the host of the Lord. This was an anxious time for Joshua. There was no going back; the bridges were burned. "When Joshua was near Jericho, he looked up" (v. 13). I ask myself as I look at this story, what is Joshua doing? Is he praying? Is he saying, "Oh, God, what are we going to do? You promised that you'd be with me but there's that city. I don't know how we're going to get through it. I don't know how we're going to go around this place. We can't go back." Is he meditating? Or is he trying to check the enemies' defenses, to see what he has to overcome?

Scripture says he "looked up and saw a man . . . with a drawn sword in his hand" (v. 13). Joshua asks the man if he's friend or foe. And the man's reply is that He is the Commander of all the forces! God Himself! Joshua learned

59

a lesson then and there. Joshua learned that he must submit.

Once again it is the old story of obedience. Obedience and reverence are due to God. God, as the Commander of the army, bears the responsibility. We know that we are engaged in a holy war. The battle is the Lord's, but we must not forget to do our part. Joshua was doing what he was supposed to do. He was worshiping and doing his duty. And that is when God appeared.

Three angels came down to commune with Abraham. Lot was nearby, but they did not commune with Lot; they communed with Abraham (see Gen. 18). God was seen with the three Hebrews in the fiery furnace, but Nebuchadnezzar did not see Him in Babylon (see Dan. 3:23-25). God reveals Himself to people who love Him and walk with Him. The two disciples who were on the road to Emmaus saw the risen Christ (see Luke 24:13-31). The Scripture says, "Come near to God and he will come near to you" (Jas. 4:8).

Joshua was doing what God wanted Him to do. Be encouraged by that. Keep on doing the thing God has put before you. Keep on fulfilling your duty. Keep on trusting what God has put before you at this time, and He will take care of the rest. Those know best how to command, who know best how to obey.

Joshua was being fitted by God to be the leader of God's people. The Captain of the host of the Lord came to him, and Joshua fell on his face and worshiped Him. Joshua asked the Captain, "What message does my Lord have for his servant?" (v. 14).

Here Joshua comes face-to-face with the One whom Revelation calls the King of kings the Lord of lords; the One who commands the unseen army. Jacob saw that unseen army. Elijah's servant saw that army. Jesus said He could command that army to come from heaven to deliver Him. Joshua fell on his face and worshiped this Commander. He was ready to obey His command, to follow His leadership. You ought also to allow yourself to accept His leadership, to fall at His feet. And as you do, watch those modern walls of Jericho come tumbling down.

Follow the Leader! That is the secret to power. That is the secret to an overcoming victorious life. As the work of God is put before us, so is His help. Jesus said, "Apart from me you can do nothing" (John 15:5). That is true. When He commands, He also assists.

Here God reveals Himself to Joshua. He reveals Himself in a variety of ways to meet the needs of us all. He is known as the Good Shepherd, the Great Physician, the Carpenter, the Saviour.

Joshua was standing at the edge of the greatest experience in his life. He had come through some mighty and powerful things, but now he was facing the greatest kind of barrier he had ever faced—the whole city of Jericho. But the Captain of the host of the Lord came, and Joshua fell on his face to worship Him. Joshua said, "Lord, what will you have me to do?" And the Captain responded, "Take off your sandals, for the place where you are standing is holy" (see Josh. 5:14,15).

Are you in that sort of relationship to God? If you are, the invisible army of God is available to you for a resource and for power. Fall before God as your Commander and say, "Lord, I'll do what you want me to do."

The Conquest of Jericho
The conquest of Jericho is the center of the drama. Everything prior to this is preparation for it. Jericho was

the central fortified city of all the Canaanites. It was a powerful fortress. It was an obstacle that barred the Israelites from the Promised Land. The city of Jericho, with all its fortifications, stood between the people of God and that land which He promised them so long ago.

According to Joshua 6:1, Jericho was under siege; there was no activity going back and forth. The city was locked up.

The Canaanites were in deep trouble, but they did not suddenly come to that place. God knew these people for a long time; they are mentioned in Genesis 10:18. One particular group of these people—those who lived in Sodom—*"were* wicked and sinners before the Lord" (Gen. 13:13, *KJV*); already we see the deterioration of these people. Genesis 19:1-28 tells the story of God's judgment on the Canaanites of Sodom and Gomorrah.

Judgment did not just suddenly open up and fall out of the sky upon the Canaanites. The people were deteriorating in their moral and spiritual lives and they had been warned by God many times. Remember what happened down in Egypt before the Israelites left. Do not think that news of that did not get up to the land of Canaan! Rumors spread as rapidly in Joshua's day as they do today. The people knew something horrible was going on down in the land of Egypt. They certainly were not surprised when a cloud of dust appeared across the Jordan, in the lower part of the sandy desert. They had heard for 40 years that the people of God were wandering around in that desert.

God was working out His purposes through the people of Israel and the Canaanites should have known it. They should have understood that the things that were happening were warnings and signs. For 450 years God had been patient. He continued to lead His people; His hand was upon them throughout their history. Their experiences served as illustrations for other people, particularly for the Canaanites who once had a very close relationship with God before they wandered away.

For the past 40 years the Canaanites watched the cloud of threat grow darker, and now it hung over Jericho. They could not go in and they could not go out of their own city. There is a warning here for all nations, including our own. Things do not just keep going along the same way. We ought to learn that the things that happen speak to us of God's purposes. God has been patient, but God will not be patient forever. "Seek the Lord while he may be found; call on him while he is near" (Isa. 55:6).

The vengeance about to fall upon Jericho is not a private one that belongs only to Israel. It is God's righteous judgment of a people whose iniquity has become full (compare Gen. 15:16).

The Canaanites must have sensed their coming judgment for they were paralyzed with fear. Their only hope lay in the strength of their city wall. That is a precarious position. You're better off marching in a silent crowd with the blessing of God than cowering behind 10-foot walls without that blessing.

Jericho was one of the great walled cities described by the Israelite spies 40 years before (see Num. 13:28). Now the next generation of Israelites stood facing the walls that their fathers were so worried about. But God makes the difference, and the walls of the city of Jericho are not going to hold back the purposes of God.

We Have to Do Our Part
Chapter 6 of Joshua has some important lessons in it for us. Verses 2-21 show us our part in life's battles. Spur-

geon used to say that God wants His people to work, to wait and to win. God has work for His people to do, but He also gives them a promise. Verse 2 says, "I have delivered Jericho into your hands." That is a good thing to know!

There it stood in all its awesomeness, with its staunch walls. "How in the world are we going to get through the city of Jericho?" the people of Israel probably asked. How do desert nomads crush a fortress? They do it by the promise of God. That promise is theirs to stand by and to stand on. And verses 3-5 show that God expects activity on the part of His people. Here is the active side to Christian warfare—it is not all passive. Once every day these thousands of armed men were to walk around the walls of Jericho. God's promises do not lead to inactivity. God always gives faith plenty of things to do. We are not to sit idly by quoting verses and hope we can be excused for our inactivity.

We have the promises of God but those promises never lead to idleness. There are instructions in the Bible for conquest and if we are to achieve the victories God has for us, then we must work at them. We are faithfully to discharge our responsibility but we are to do this by employing God's methods and His means.

Sometimes we do not know what God's way is and often it is a very difficult thing to determine, but the Lord will honor our efforts and our desire to do things His way. However, when we are doing God's work merely in the strength of our own ability, God says He cannot let that be.

It is important to know God's way. Joshua was not free to follow his own plan; he had to strictly keep the word of the Lord. God did not just say, "Joshua, there's the Promised Land, go to it." God said, "There's the Promised

Land, Joshua, but this is the way you get across the River Jordan; and here are explicit directions as to what you're supposed to do." And Joshua did what God said. We also have a responsibility to work in the light of the promises of God and do it God's way.

We Have to Obey

The second thing about our work is that it is to be done in reverent obedience. In Joshua 6:6-9, Joshua explains God's plan to the people. They were to march silently around the city once a day for a week. I suspect that as they followed God's strange instructions on the first day they could easily see that nothing happened. Maybe somebody said on the second day, "I don't see a thing different." Perhaps by the time they got along toward the end of the week, many people were saying, "What are we doing? The city's still there, the walls haven't even begun to come down." There was not much progress and not much evidence of blessing. The walls were still there.

The activists in the group probably said, "Let's *do* something instead of just walking around this town." But remember, they had their orders and their orders were to do precisely as they were doing now. It must have seemed foolish; it certainly would appear so to the people who were watching them. The people in the city of Jericho must have looked on the Israelites' march as a ridiculous procedure. So it is in much of the world today. The world sees much of Christian work and much of Christian faith as foolish.

How often do you hear people of the world, as they look on the things of the gospel, say, "What a waste of time! What a waste of a life!" Many people have said to me, in reference to those who give themselves to some

65

kind of full-time activity for God, "What a waste of good talent and ability." Perhaps this is what it looks like. We spend a lot of our time marching around the walls of language training, marching around the walls of preparation for service. But we must keep at it. God said this is the way victory will ultimately be achieved.

Parents sometimes feel that they have been wasting their time marching around the walls of faithfully trying to teach children and instruct them in the ways of the Lord. Christians sometimes complain that it is a waste of time to walk around the walls of obedience to God. But these are our orders. God told us precisely what we are to do and we had better do it.

There is a call for reverent obedience on the part of God's people. Part of this is so that God may receive the glory. Victory must never be ascribed to ourselves. Our responsibility is to reverently obey, to walk around those walls as God leads us.

Another lesson begins in verse 10: "Joshua had commanded the people, 'Do not give a war cry, do not raise your voices, do not say a word until the day I tell you to shout. Then shout!'" There is in the battle of life a place of silence and trust. The people were instructed to be still. The Bible speaks about that in other places. "Stand firm and you will see the deliverance the Lord will bring you today" (Exod. 14:13). "The Lord is in his holy temple; let all the earth be silent before him" (Hab. 2:20). "Do not be quick with your mouth, do not be hasty in your heart to utter anything before God. God is in heaven and you are on earth, so let your words be few" (Eccles. 5:2). Maybe we ought to review these verses everyday. Certainly the implications are overwhelming.

Our Lord Jesus Christ is our pattern in silent obedience. He endured when He had no place to lay His head; when He knew that even His brethren did not believe on Him; when He saw the apostles deny Him; when He entered the agony of Gethsemane; when He was despised and rejected of men. Yet Scripture says He opened not His mouth (see Isa. 53:7). He trusted God.

We Have to Wait

There is a third thing we must do—wait. Joshua and the Israelites waited a whole week. A week is not a very long time in some instances but it is interminable in others. This must have seemed a very long week. A week of suffering mockery and ridicule, of wondering what would happen.

Many of the promises of the Bible call for patience on our part. "Blessed are all who wait for him," Isaiah tells us (Isa. 30:18). "Trust in the Lord with all your heart" (Prov. 3:5). "Commit your way to the Lord; trust in him" (Ps. 37:5). You will keep in perfect peace him whose mind is steadfast, because he trusts in you" (Isa. 26:3). We have a part in the battles of life, and one aspect of that is waiting.

But the Israelites discovered that the results were worth waiting for. The long week of enduring ridicule, of walking around the wall without seeing any results, was over. "On the seventh day, they got up at daybreak and marched around the city seven times in the same manner, except that on that day they circled the city seven times. The seventh time around, when the priests sounded the trumpet blast, Joshua commanded the people, 'Shout! For the LORD has given you the city!' . . . When the trumpets sounded, the people shouted, and at the sound of the trumpet, when the people gave a loud shout, the wall collapsed" (Josh. 6:15,16,20).

67

Our Problem Is Ourselves

There is a final lesson in this conquest of Jericho. The real battle about which we are reading is not with the Canaanites at all. It is with God's own people! What a jolt this brought to me when I realized that all of this organization, all of this marching, all of this blowing of trumpets, all of this numerical listing of sevens, were not really necessary to knock down a little wall. God was not frantically collecting His energy so that He could destroy Jericho. He could have just spoken and Jericho would have vaporized. After all, didn't God just speak a word and worlds sprang into existence? His power was not limited to a few people walking around a city and blowing trumpets.

The real battle of Jericho was with the human heart, not with the wall of the city. God was seeking to overcome the Israelites rather than simply to overcome the Canaanites. God was seeking to subdue the Israelites to Himself, to bind them with cords of faith and love. In the same way, God could have staggered the world with a word. But instead, He asks us to choose Him and to prefer His will to our own.

There is always a Jericho. You face it in your own life. Sometimes it is within, a weakness, a constant temptation with which you struggle. You know what it is that you are prone to do or fall before. This you must conquer, for this is your Jericho.

Your Jericho may be something on the outside. It may be a family situation, it may be a circumstance that fights to hold you back from doing what you know God wants you to do. These walls also will fall only by faith. Learn that it is God who must bring about this accomplishment. It is too big for you and for me. There is too much to overcome. But God's omnipotent resources are there. We try to bat-

68

ter down the walls of our Jerichos with our preaching, with our committees and our plans. These are useful only if God is pleased to touch them. Trust Him, obey Him, wait for Him!

Footnote

1. Alan Redpath, *Victorious Christian Living* (Old Tappan: Fleming H. Revell Company, 1955), p. 77.

6
Disobedience Equals Defeat

Joshua 7,8

If I had written the book of Joshua, I would have left out chapter 7. It is an uncomfortable chapter. It dashes cold water on our experiences. It is like finding the serpent in the Garden of Eden. It ruins everything. Finding Achan in Israel is like discovering Judas among the disciples. But we can learn something from it.

The people had a marvelous victory at Jericho. God said they were not to take any booty for themselves, but were to set aside certain valuables for the treasury of the Lord (see Josh. 6:18,19). But Achan, in direct violation of what God said, chose to keep some things. He found a beautiful garment and some pieces of silver and gold so attractive to him that he took them and hid them in his tent. No one else knew about it, but suddenly calamity came crashing down on the people of God. Israel was humiliated and defeated at Ai.

Joshua went into a state of depression, fell on his face and said, "If only we had been content to stay on the other side of the Jordan!" God said, "Stand up! What are you doing down on your face? Israel has sinned . . . I will not be with you anymore unless you destroy whatever among you is devoted to destruction." (Josh. 7:7,10-12).

That is what happened. Lots were cast in some fashion. Joshua worked his way through the tribes, families, households and individuals until the lot rested by divine appointment upon Achan. It was not until that point, when he was caught red-handed, that Achan finally said, "It is true! I have sinned against the Lord" (Josh. 7:20), and the judgment of God fell upon him.

Now let us go back to verse 1. The first sentence gives a danger signal. The children of Israel committed a sin, a trespass. One of them, Achan, saw what God said he was not to take, and took it anyway. So God said, "All right, I'll have to lift my blessing."

It is startling to read in the latter part of verse 1 that God was angry. "The LORD'S anger burned against Israel." God is described to us again and again as a God of great compassion and a God of love. But do not overlook the other characteristic described for us in Scripture: God has the capacity to become angry.

Stay Close to God

Time after time in the Old Testament, when the people of God insisted on wandering away from the will of God, the displeasure of God was revealed. Anytime there was disobedience by the people of God, there was judgment.

We see in Joshua, as well as in other places, the great principle of the devastating, separating power of sin. Sin always disintegrates, sin always breaks unity. It breaks the unity of the peace in a person's heart, in a community, in the world. It can break the unity of the family, the church and partnerships.

When sin comes into your life, your church or your relationships, it always results in some kind of a rout, a defeat. When God departs from the scene, as God departed from the scene at Ai, defeat is the natural thing to expect.

Verses 2-4 tell one of the saddest parts of the whole story. Joshua gives his instructions to the people as if everything were all right. He is going along blindly ignorant of the fact that God—the Captain of the host, the One who has said, "I will be with you as I was with Moses," the One who made possible the crossing of the Jordan River, the One who knocked down the walls of Jericho—is no longer with His people to help them against Ai. What a frightening thing. Joshua does not know that the power has been withdrawn, that God has departed. Whether Joshua should have sensed the problem or not you will have to decide.

I do not know of any more sad or depressing experiences in the Bible than the times when men who had enjoyed the blessing of God discovered to their great sadness that that blessing had been lifted. Remember Saul and those awful words, "The Spirit of the LORD had departed from Saul" (1 Sam. 16:14). That is a terrifying and frightening prospect.

There were times in the history of these people when Moses said, "Do not go up (to fight), because the LORD is not with you" (Num. 14:42). It is a good thing to be aware of that *before* you launch yourself into a battle where your only hope is the Lord. Moses apparently was sensitive to the presence of God in such a way that he could say to the

72

people, "Don't go now; this is the wrong time for you to start a battle, for God is not in your midst."

Perhaps the clearest and most sobering illustration of this is the story of Samson. Here was a man who was given unusual strength and an important mission by God. But he let himself be sidetracked by his fancy for Delilah. She wormed his secret out of him after several efforts, and then she let the Philistines shave his head and thus deprive him of his strength. When he woke up, he said, "'I'll go out as before and shake myself free.' But he did not know that the LORD had left him" (Judg. 16:20). He did not know that God had lifted His blessing.

To be doing God's work is no guarantee of having God's help. There is a principle for us here—do not move until God says so. Yesterday's blessings are not enough for us today. Stay close to the Lord, so that you can sense His presence.

Stay Pure in the Body

This portion of our study also illustrates another truth. One man can be the means of holding up the blessing of God. We hear a great deal today about Body Life, with the emphasis upon the unity of God's people. This is a scriptural emphasis. And when we translate that analogy over into the context of our present text, we can see how the influence of one person can be detrimental. It is possible that one member of the Body can be corrupt. As Paul points out in 1 Corinthians 5:6, a little leaven influences the whole system. Or again, in 1 Corinthians 12:26 we read, "And whether one member suffer, all the members suffer with it; or one member be honored, all the members rejoice with it" (KJV). Here is a clear and clarion call for purity within the Body of Christ.

73

Then, as the passage goes on to point out, this very trying and difficult experience in the lives of the people of God led to a time of prayer. There is a call in Scripture for the experience of godly sorrow. This was the time to undergo that. People began also to have some considerable doubt of what God was doing in their midst. And of course it is very easy to come to this place. How often have you suggested, "The Lord has let me down!"? Now perhaps we do not say that openly, but we surely do feel that from time to time. The psalmist expressed this fear on a number of occasions when he felt that God was not with him at the moment when he needed Him! It is so easy to question. When the darkness falls around us it is hard to remember what the light was like. When ill health settles in upon us, it is hard to remember those long years of good health.

Then, as a result of the prayer time, you will note in verses 10-15, God graciously and faithfully gives instruction. Prayer always brings enlightenment and instruction. Prayer in the history of the people of God always brought for them His guidance. Prayer prepared them for what was going to happen to them and for that which they must do. My friend, there are times when we had better stop everything and pray! There is no sense in doubling the force or renewing the efforts when what we really need to do is to pray. The Lord has graciously provided this means of making Himself known and of guiding His people. Let us be sure that we are taking advantage of Him fully.

Be Aware of Disobedience

Now move down in the chapter to verse 26 and carefully read it. It says to us, "They heaped up a large pile of rocks, which remains to this day." Here is a monument to one man's disobedience. We see monuments scattered throughout the pages of the Old Testament. What are some of the lessons that come to us through this particular monument?

First, we see here the need for developing a deep consciousness of sin's existence and the awfulness of being guilty of offending God. As we wait increasingly in God's presence, we become increasingly aware of sin. Christians who have walked the way of faith for years will testify again and again that the closer they come to the things of the Lord, the more offensive sin becomes. We are urged in Scripture not even to entertain sin's possibilities. We are warned in Scripture to avoid the very appearance of evil. Someone suggested that we are to "kill it before it kills us." We are challenged in Scripture to live above it and beyond it. This is not a plea for perfectionism but a strong reminder that we are to strive against sin and evil. We must be alert.

And furthermore, we are taught in this context to beware of self-confidence. The smallest temptations become too much for us. We need to learn with the apostle Paul that, "For when I am weak, then I am strong" (2 Cor. 12:10). We need the strength of God for every battle. We must not be guilty of presumption. The moment of victory in our experience is the moment of renewed caution, and for renewed trust. God simply will not condone sin in His own people.

The second lesson we can learn from this monument is that we are all in this battle together! I do not believe this is an emphasis of corporate guilt or of community guilt. We are often accused of being responsible for that which our forefathers have done in the past. It is true, as Scripture tells us, that the sins of the fathers indeed can be visited

75

upon the children. But actually being responsible for what someone said or did a long time ago is a slightly different matter.

So, though there may not be emphasis here upon community guilt, we are charged with the responsibility of aiding each other. I have often asked myself as I have read this passage, "Did anyone help Achan overcome his temptation to disobey God?" To be sure, it was a deliberate and a purposive determination. We see this on other occasions in Scripture, for example in the book of Acts, where Ananias and Sapphira determined they would rebel against God. Or, back in the Old Testament again, we see where David determined that he was going to send Uriah into the forefront of the battle in the hopes that he would be killed. But the questions still remain: What was the influence of other people in the camp? Had anyone determined that he would set a good example for Achan?

I am well aware that it is very difficult to know when to intervene, and when things must be left to the Lord. But there does seem to be something in this paragraph that teaches us the need for sensitivity and responsibility as it relates to our fellow believers. There is something about the whole Church that is brought into purview here and reminds us that we are indeed our brother's keeper.

Another lesson that stands out here is the fact that there is a day coming when all mankind will stand before the Lord God. He has taught us in Scripture that He is indeed the Judge of all the earth. Even as Achan stood before Joshua and was judged for his action, so the whole world must face the same prospect. At that time, Scripture tells us the sheep will be separated from the goats; the hidden things of darkness will be brought to light. And oh, what a joy it is to know that our sins indeed are forgiven and that our destiny is settled forever and forever because of our faith in the living Christ.

One final thing needs to be mentioned: we are taught in the New Testament the joy of forgiveness. We are told in Scripture that we are to confess to God and forsake our sins. This poor man Achan touched the life of Israel and by his action hindered the whole nation. He was guilty of taking what belonged to God. We must all admit that we have done the same. We all have taken things that belong only to the Lord: His glory, His honor, a clear witness for His name. Oh, that we would then bring to Him all that has been displeasing and evil and wrong and cast it at His feet and determine to give it up and let Him destroy all that may be contrary to His perfect will!

This is a difficult chapter in Scripture. In it, we have seen the anger of God. We have been warned again what a terrible thing it is to fall out of fellowship with the living, righteous and the holy God. We see the weakness of our own humanity. Once again we are called to cast ourselves upon the mercy of the Lord and ask for His grace, forgiveness and cleansing power and the strength that is needed to carry out His purposes day by day.

Victory Restored

When we come to Joshua 8 it is as though we were coming out of a dark night into the brilliance of sunlight. There is a whole new perspective now, a whole new turn of events, a whole new atmosphere. It is not that chapter 7 is to be forgotten as if it were a bad dream, or written off as a page in history that one would rather forget. Rather, in keeping with the instructions and the information that come to us out of chapter 7, we can move into chapter 8 and its new instructions to us.

Verse 1 gives us a fairly clear outline of the whole chapter.

First, there is an assurance of comfort, "The Lord said unto Joshua, 'Do not be afraid; do not be discouraged.'" Second, it gives a clarity of instruction: "Take the whole army with you, and go up and attack Ai." Third, there is the promise of victory: "I have delivered into your hands the king of Ai."

God Gives Comfort

First let us look at the assurance of comfort. "The Lord said unto Joshua, 'Do not be afraid; do not be discouraged.'" We do not always get a second chance, but sometimes in the mercy and the providence of God, we do. One of my favorite texts is in the book of Jonah. The first two chapters tell of Jonah's disobedience to God, his flight and his experience with the fish. Then chapter 3 begins with this expression: "Then the word of the LORD came to Jonah a second time" (Jon. 3:1). That is a great expression! I am grateful for those times when God in His mercy feels that we can be trusted with a second chance.

The Israelites had plenty of reason to fear, so when God came along and said, "Do not be afraid," that was good news. God had judged them; He had withheld blessings. That was a fearful, frightening thing, for they were just beginning this entrance into the Promised Land and they knew full well that if the blessing of God did not go with them they would never make it. There had been mass confusion, so much so that the leaders flung themselves on their faces in the dust and said, "Lord, what shall we do?" I suspect this struck terror in the hearts of the people.

Then there was that dreadful scene when Achan and

his family were stoned to death, and finally, the mound of rocks raised over the victims. Those people learned that corruption within is the worst kind of corruption.

The trouble was *within*. The main trouble was not the strong army of opposition out there but the opposition inside the camp. That internal problem had to be straightened out before the blessing of God could be anticipated in any further efforts. But the people also learned that God is able to forgive. That is more than we are able to do sometimes, either for ourselves or for other people.

A painter named William Blake once painted a beautiful but strong and vicious tiger. Then he wrote some lines in which he asked, "Did He who made the lamb make thee?" We have to admit that sometimes the God of the tiger seems as one God and the God of the lamb another. So chapter 7 portrays God and chapter 8 portrays God. All of life shows us the startling differences in the characteristics of God. This is one of the things over which we really do some inner struggling. The God of spring and plenty and health sometimes seems so different from the God of winter and famine and sickness. He is the God of children's joys and laughter, but He is also God when that laughter is stilled.

In chapter 7 we read of a God who was greatly to be feared. But in chapter 8 we see another side of God—the side which is to be loved and joyfully served. It does seem to me that there is one thing we must learn out of all of this: God loves us *always*. Whatever the human predicament in which we find ourselves, *God loves us* in the midst of it all.

We are often at peace when we should fear. We often fear when we should be at peace. Someone said it is not the contrite man but the unrepentant man who has cause to fear that God will turn against him. The Pharisee may cower before the words of Christ, but the woman in tears at His feet may trust Him and not be afraid. God is a complex Being. We must not be guilty of oversimplifying Him as a kind of a great big grandfather in the heavens who looks down with worry and concern over the battlements every now and then, and wrings His hands in nervous agitation over what is going on. Unfortunately, that is the picture a lot of people have of God.

Others see Him as some kind of dreadful giant, who longs to put people through their paces, to see how tough He can make it for them. Or He is seen as a very soft, sentimental kind of Person who would not harm a fly, so there is no reason for anybody to be concerned about what He has to say.

But if you study Scripture, you will always come out of chapter 7 into chapter 8. You will find that God has a side that is greatly to be feared, but He is also the One who says to us, "Do not be afraid. Do not be discouraged." Our Lord Jesus Christ wept over the city of Jerusalem and then, with the tears hardly dry upon His cheeks, He stormed into the Temple and cleansed it! (See Luke 19:41,45,46.) Scripture describes the contrasting personality traits of God.

The joy of Joshua chapter 8 is forgiveness and pardon. "As far as the east is from the west, so far has he removed our transgressions from us" (Ps. 103:12). God cast our sins behind Him. He will remember them against us no more. We may well be ashamed of our transgressions, but we need not fear to meet God, for His forgiveness is complete and He has washed the record clean.

With forgiveness, confidence is restored and we can go on. Oh, we have learned—painfully and sometimes in a crushing way—that God is sensitive to sin. And God will judge it. But we have also learned that to every penitent sinner, to every penitent believer, He says, "Your sins, which are many, are all forgiven. Go in peace" (see Luke 7:47,48,50). That is part of the good news of the gospel. That is one of the reasons it is referred to as good news. The experiences of Joshua 7 can lead us into the good news of Joshua 8, that says, "Do not be afraid. Do not be discouraged."

God Gives Instruction

The second point is the clarity of instruction: "Take the whole army with you, and go up and attack Ai." The third verse reveals that 30,000 soldiers were assigned to the task force to go and capture Ai. That is a far cry from the original group of 3,000 that started out for Ai in chapter 7. It is important that we get clear instructions from God, and Joshua apparently failed to do this the first time.

There is another lesson here. It is more difficult to find your way back after you have sinned than it would have been if you had not gone wrong in the first place. It was so much trouble to overthrow Ai—it took an army of 30,000 men. I do not know what it would have been before if they had listened to God's instructions, but we can certainly see what is going to happen now. This was just a little town. It was not any Jericho. But it took 30,000 men and some very clever tactics to capture it.

Many believers learn that it is costly to leave the path of blessing. It is so tragic to go off the track because it is so hard to get back on. The longer people stay off, the harder it is to get back on the right track. That is a principle that is working its way right through our society.

I do not mean that people cannot come back—they

81

can. And thank God they do. The power of the gospel is sufficient for any person's need. But lost ground is very difficult to regain. Backsliding, as the old-timers used to call it, is simply disobedience. It is being out of fellowship with God. We are warned about it again and again. God graciously and faithfully tries to tell us the costs of moving away from His will.

Scripture says not to lean on your own understanding (see Prov. 3:5). Do not be guided simply by your own self-will. We all know people who have been waylaid—people who have been shunted off the track, who have wasted years—and sometimes never do get back because the cost is too high. I meet people all the time who suggest this to me. People say, "I used to go to church and Sunday School when I was a kid, but no more. I was once a Christian, but I gave it all up. My parents were too fundamentalistic—had too strict a code in our house—so I threw it all over." What these comments usually mean—and I do not say this unkindly—is that the speaker has a wandering heart, an indiscretion somewhere along the line, a strong self-will. What he is really saying is, "It isn't my mother and father that have driven me away from this—it's me. I don't want to come back. The cost is too high."

It's a hard road back. But it is a trip we must take. Jacob had to go back to Bethel where he first met God. He had to get rid of all the pagan gods and idols and other things that were cluttering up his family life (see Gen. 35:1-3). If need be, we too must go back to Bethel—back to the place where we began to stray from God's road.

Another lesson I see here is that there is biblical support for the old saying, "If at first you don't succeed, try, try again." God is saying to His people, "Head back to the battlefield. Don't quit because you've suffered a setback. Don't quit because you've been wounded." Micah 7:8 says, "Do not gloat over me, my enemy! Though I have fallen, I will rise." Get back on your feet spiritually. Get back on God's road for your life. You may have fallen, but all is not lost. Listen to God's instruction. He has a message for you. That message is, "Arise and go! Do what I tell you to do"; whatever the past, get out of chapter 7 and get into chapter 8. Press on in obedience to the call of God.

God Promises Victory

The third thing we find in the first verse is a promise of victory. God said, "I have delivered into your hands the king of Ai." We Christians should live in the light of the promises of God, and let those promises permeate every situation in which we find ourselves. Here is our ground of freedom from fear. We can meet the giant enemies of life with the weapons God has provided for us. God wants His children to have victory. He doesn't want us to live a defeated and crushed life but one that is victorious and overcoming. The psalmist said, "When I am afraid, I will trust in you" (Ps. 56:3).

Take the armor of God and get back into the battle with the assurance and the confidence that God is saying, "I have given you the land."

We are to trust the promises and exercise faith, but we also have a duty in this Christian life business. These people had to go and fight. So do we. The Christian life is described as a battle—and it is! Fight, then, for that which is right. Fight against temptation. Fight against the time-consuming things that would crowd in upon you and destroy your priorities. Fight to discover God's will for your life. Fight to be a loving, kind and understanding person. Fight the discouragement that creeps in and paralyzes you. Fight that personality weakness that has dogged you all the days of your life.

"I have given you the king of Ai and his people and his city and his land. Now you go out there and do your duty," is what God said. The assurances of victory are yours and the provisions for a successful fight belong to you. "Trust in the Lord with all your heart and lean not on your own understanding; in all your ways acknowledge him, and he will make your paths straight" (Prov. 3:5,6). There's good news in the power of the gospel that will enable us to be free from fear and to enjoy the victory God has for His people.

Preparing for Battle

The people who were the enemy of God's people had many fine characteristics: they were full of zeal; they were enthusiastic; they were determined. The men of Ai got up early—they were not slothful; they had an army—they were not ill-prepared; they were committed to defend the city of Ai—they were patriotic, loyal, deeply committed. But more than these things were needed for victory. Earnestness and zeal are fine characteristics, and many people have these characteristics. But they are not enough in the battles of life.

The people who were the enemies of God's people were brave. They took many wise precautions. They had the general support of all the people. But there was one thing they did not have: the right relationship with God. And this one lack determined the game right from the beginning.

Joshua Acts on Instructions

Joshua was a strategist. Of course, he had the advantage of receiving directions from God. As soon as Joshua knew what he was supposed to do, he did it. In his speech to his soldiers he had one goal in mind: to perform what God commanded. This is not a new thing for Joshua, but it is reemphasized in the light of the great difficulty the people had fallen into when the blessing of God was removed. Joshua stressed the need to do what God told them to do (see Josh. 8:8). He was exercising faith, and he was standing on the authority he derived from God.

In verses 14 through 17 you will find a description of the battle of Ai. The strategy was to plant part of the army in ambush near the city wall. The rest of the army, with Joshua, would march toward the city, prepared for combat. When the king of Ai saw the army of Joshua coming again, he would throw open the gates of the city and lead his soldiers to battle. Joshua and his army would pretend they were being beaten and flee, with the enemy army in pursuit. Then the army in ambush would run into the city, take it and set it on fire. And that is exactly what happened. Israel destroyed the city and achieved complete victory.

What is the lesson we can learn from this part of Joshua? The people of Ai were convinced they were right; they were enthusiastic; they were full of zeal; they were willing to give themselves in devotion. But they needed light to guide them in the truth and the people of Ai did not have that light. Truth, not majority, is the guideline for our lives. It may mean that sometimes we stand in left field by ourselves. But that is a safe place to be if it is on the solid ground of truth. Now in further review of this ambush you will see that Joshua holds out his spear (see v. 18). Perhaps this had a symbolic meaning. It may have been a picture of supplication or it may have been a picture of prayer. Nevertheless, as he holds out his spear the battle progresses.

This must have been a great reminder to Joshua of something that had happened 40 years before at a town called Rephidim. This time Joshua was on the field of battle and Moses was watching. At Rephidim, Moses had held up his hands, and as long as his hands were up the battle progressed. When his hands got tired and fell, the battle went against Israel. Aaron and Hur finally had to hold his hands up so that Israel could win the battle (see Exod. 17:11,12). Now 40 years later Joshua is in a similar situation. He finds that as long as he holds out his spear, Israel prospers in the battle.

When we have needs, and we trust God to work out His good pleasure, those needs will be met at the right time. Remember the story of Hagar? She was despised by her mistress Sarah, so she fled. She was found by an angel of the Lord at the right time, under the right circumstances (see Gen. 16:6-9). When Elijah reached a low point in his life, God fed and protected him in a supernatural way (see 1 Kings 19:5-7). Peter was delivered from prison at just the right time (see Acts 12:7-10). Paul and Silas at Philippi were wonderfully delivered by the grace and intervention of God (see Acts 16:24-28,35-40).

The hand of God, though invisible, will bring relief to those who fear Him. We can rejoice and find great confidence and assurance in that knowledge. But we have to look at the other side of the coin too. Hebrews 11 tells of the marvelous intervention of God on behalf of His people in many cases throughout biblical history. But the chapter goes on to tell of another type of experience. "Some faced jeers and flogging . . . . They were stoned; they were sawed in two; they were put to death by the sword" (Heb. 11:36,37). Some were delivered; some were not. Whether we are delivered or not, we are all the objects of His care.

Whether or not God delivers us from our trials, nothing takes away the truth of God's continued loving care for you and me. Do not let your understanding of the love of God depend upon whether or not you have perfect health or the degree of success in your life. God, in His providence, in His mercy and in the overall purposes of His love, has seen fit to raise up some; others He has not raised up. But that does not make Him any less a powerful or loving God. And that does not mean that you have any less reason to trust Him or that you should have any doubt or fear in your heart that God loves you. He has promised to care for His own.

Joshua Builds an Altar

After the successful campaign against Ai, Joshua builds an altar (see Josh. 8:30). Once more there is a ceremony of renewal. We read about an altar that Abraham built in Genesis 12. We read about other altars in Moses' time, and now Joshua builds an altar. Each time the people of God built an altar they recognized it as a time of renewal. Such times happen again and again in Scripture and how we thank God for that. God is pleased to bring renewal again and again to His Church.

There was a renewal of the covenant of God at Gilgal. We read that in Joshua 1. Exodus 31:16 talks about the observance of the Sabbath day as a perpetual covenant. Every act of worship, I believe, is a time of renewal. Here in Joshua they stopped what they were doing, and they put first things first. There is a time to do battle, but there is also a time to worship and to pray. And we need discernment from God to understand which is which.

The altar is further evidence of obedience. Back in Deuteronomy 11:29-32, Moses said that when the Israelites crossed the River Jordan, they should go between the two mountains, Ebal and Gerizim. That is exactly where they are geographically in Joshua chapter 8. This is in obedience to God. It may have seemed to be a risky and unnatural thing to go 20 or 30 miles north into enemy territory to encamp in order to worship God. But 40 years of experience taught the people of God that they had no reason to fear anything God commanded.

From the Red Sea to Ai there is one continuous illustration of how safe it is to do the will of God. In the will of God the Red Sea became a wall of water on either side, and it stood there long enough for safety; then it fell on the enemies of God.

But outside the will of God a handful of men from a little town called Ai brought danger and judgment to one who disobeyed God. As long as we walk in the will and practices of God we are safe. But when we step outside His will and go our own direction, we stand in danger. We are safe in His will though we may be weak; but in danger out of His will though we seem strong.

That altar Joshua builds after Ai is God's altar. Even the workmanship indicated that. There was to be no pollution. They were not to shape or cut the stones, but just take whole stones and pile them into an altar. The spiritual lesson here is that the way to God is never through human working. Salvation is never by self-effort.

The altar is not just a pile of rocks that ancient people laid down a long time ago. The altar is far more significant for us as we look at it today. It is a picture of God meeting the needs of His people.

The People Reaffirm Their Commitment

The chapter closes with an affirmation in verses 34,35. This solemn gathering concluded with the determination on the part of the people to keep God's law. The Israelites committed themselves to God's law 40 years before at Sinai, and now they reaffirmed their commitment. That is what we need to do. A successful life is built upon obedience to God's commands, and, "His commands are not burdensome" (1 John 5:3). God wants what is best for us.

The people of God rebuilt the altar, they reaffirmed their commitment to the things of their God and afterwards Joshua "read all the words of" God's Words to which they responded with a loud *Amen.*

God is still looking for people who live in obedience to Him. The *altar* and the *Word* go together. "Faith comes from hearing the message, and the message is heard through the word of Christ" (Rom. 10:17). Together, they reveal to us the King of the universe in all His power and His beauty. And this revelation and resulting obedience is for all: the leaders, the family, the strangers, the elders and the little ones.

Thus the Word of God continues to be a witness. Even as it was in the days of Joshua, so today it becomes either a blessing or a curse. We may disobey the revealed purposes of God and be miserable. We may, on the other hand, live in His purpose and be happy and useful.

7
Compromise, Survival and Grace

Joshua 9

This book of Joshua is a foreshadowing of the the spiritual warfare into which all believers are called. It is important that we recognize that it is not just a record of some interesting battles and some interesting people. It is that, but the book of Joshua has overtones that go far beyond a record of history. We need to keep our eyes open for the spiritual lessons as we go through this book.

In the New Testament, the apostle Paul refers to Christians as soldiers. We are talked about as those who are involved in an army of the Lord, as those who are caught up in a conflict, as those who are a portion of that great eternal battle of good and evil. (See, for example, 1 Cor. 14:8; 2 Cor. 10:3,4; 1 Tim. 1:18; 2 Tim. 2:3,4). There will always be opposition to the stand we take as believers. We are not dismayed or surprised when we discover those forces of opposition that are leveled against believers in Christ.

Resisting God

Joshua 9 begins on this theme of opposition. "Now when all the kings west of the Jordan heard about these things" (Josh. 9:1). These people heard about Joshua and the Israelites. It does not say what they heard. But certainly the implication is pretty clear that they heard of the people of God crossing the Jordan River and coming into the city of Jericho, into Ai, and then up to Gilgal.

The kings determined to resist what was taking place. Why should they not resist the enemy that was coming into their land and threatening their homes? But there is more to it. It was not simply a patriotic determination to keep an enemy force from coming through their land. It was apparently a resolution on the part of these leaders to go their own way, to resist God. They had a chance to do it in a different fashion. They thought about it, and they determined they would go in their own direction, in spite of the information that was brought to them and in spite of their understanding that God was at work. They knew of His power. They knew this was the way in which He was working and moving; and in spite of all this, they resolved to resist this.

It reminds me of what Pharaoh said: "Who is the Lord, that I should obey him?" (Exod. 5:2). There is something of that same spirit expressed here in Joshua 9:1,2. If we wanted to spiritualize this, we could say that it is an illustration of what the New Testament teaches about the carnal mind, for it says, "The sinful mind is hostile to God" (Rom. 8:7).

Whenever God is made known, there is resistance to Him. God has been made known to these people in Joshua 9. They knew. And then, after seriously considering what they knew, they resolved to go their own way.

God is pictured as One who is holy and as One who hates iniquity. God is pictured as One who has rules and regulations and standards by which He expects His people to live. These are the characteristics we resist. We do not mind a God who is a great and wonderful and powerful benefactor. But when we discover through His Word that God expects us to maintain certain standards—and God's standards cut across our own—then we must either submit ourselves to God's standards or resist them and say, "I'm going my own way."

When the kings heard, they gathered themselves together to fight (see vv. 1,2). The preaching of the gospel often produces the same type of reaction. Sometimes in the preaching of the gospel people say, "Yes, that's what I want, that's what I need. God has opened my eyes to see. I believe!" But that does not always happen with everyone. There are many times when people are exposed to God's standard and His way of living, and they resist. They say, "That's not for me; I'm not going to move in that direction." And so they gather themselves together to fight against God and His ways of doing things.

Jesus experienced this. He once said, "They hated me without reason" (John 15:25). It was all right when Jesus was healing the sick and feeding multitudes with free meals. But when He pointed out to those same people the cost of following Him and the need for obedience to His Lordship, they resisted. Some people seem to view the Lord as a buddy or a pal. And the Lord *can* be looked upon as a friendly, warm Being. But there are times when His demands are imposed upon us, and we have to decide whether or not we are going to acknowledge Him as Lord of our lives.

Immediately after Israel renewed their covenant with

the Lord and became aware of God's demands, the enemy kings set themselves against Him. Opposition often comes directly after spiritual blessing and revival. Do not be surprised when it happens in your life. The anger of satanic force seems to break out in its most violent way following periods of spiritual progress.

Deceitfulness of People

Verses 3-13 tell a strange story. The people from Gibeon, which is really just the next town away, pulled a trick on the Israelites: "They resorted to a ruse" (v. 4). They dressed as if they had been on a long journey, covered their animals with old coverings, carried old wineskins and dry, moldy bread and wore old shoes. They came to the Israelites and they said, "We have come from a distant country; make a treaty with us" (v. 6).

The people of Israel were forbidden by God to make treaties with any of the people of the Promised Land. They were supposed to destroy them all (see Exod. 23:32,33; Deut. 20:16-18). But they were taken in by the trick of the Gibeonites and "Joshua made a treaty of peace with them to let them live" (v. 15).

Whom can we trust these days? The padding of bills makes it a dreaded experience to get your car or your television set repaired. People cannot keep valuables in their desks in most of the major office buildings in American cities because of thievery. Employees steal and pad their expense accounts. We have bureaus of government to protect the consumer. We have to have food and drug control to assure that it is safe to eat and drink the things we buy in the grocery store and to guarantee that what the label says on the outside is reasonably honest. There are bureaus of weights and measures in every state to be sure that when we buy a gallon of gas, we are getting a gallon of gas. We have to hire people to protect us to be sure that things are the way they should be.

Thucydides, in his *History of the Peloponnesian Wars,* said there came a time when no man dared trust another man. That is a startling statement! He points out that the lowering of personal standards was a basic factor in the decline of Athenian civilization.

In this story of the trickery and deception of the Gibeonites, I think we see something of the deceitfulness of sin (see Heb. 3:13). Satan often encourages us to get into certain kinds of alliances, as was true here, and he suggests to us as believers, that that alliance would not do any harm. He questions the need for complete consecration. He says again and again, "Why, my friends, this is a liberated day. You are set free from the do's and don'ts of that old-fashioned religion that your parents talked about. You are no longer bound by those old-fashioned ideas."

Satan is out to do us all in. And he'll use every trick and every form of deceit he can. Be aware of his tactics—be on your guard. Satan will bring in the Gibeonites wherever possible. He will bring them into your heart, into your home, right into the church if he can. You will find evidence of those Gibeonite tendencies in your own heart. "The heart is deceitful above all things" (Jer. 17:9).

Disregard of Counsel

The Israelites were taken in by the Gibeonites because they did not ask for God's guidance. They "did not inquire of the LORD" (Josh. 9:14). Is that not amazing? Joshua and the people are just now recovering from one fiasco that almost inundated them, the defeat at Ai. They got in trouble at Ai because they did not seek God's mind;

they rushed off on their own. They said, "We don't need an army to go up there. A few people can take care of it, for it's only a small town." They did not seek the will of God.

Finally, God, in His mercy, lifted the judgment. The people got back on their feet, they had a revival and the blessing of God was upon them. Yet we go into the next chapter and find the same thing taking place again. Will we ever learn? They did not ask the counsel of the Lord. They were willing to run ahead on their own. They were back at it again.

It is so important for us to know the mind of God, to faithfully inquire of Him what He wants us to do. Some Christians say, "I want to do the will of God, but I don't know what it is." I identify with that, and I am confident the Lord understands that. At least we are asking to know what God's will is. I believe when we leave ourselves distinctly open to what God would have us do, then the responsibility is on Him to show us what we should do.

Do not be rushed into doing anything until you know the will of God for it. If you are urged to act immediately, it would be a good idea for you to back off a bit and begin to see what God says about it. "Stand still and wait" is still good advice.

In the Old Testament you have that strange expression, the Urim and the Thummim (see Exod. 28:30; Ezra 2:63). Scholars have had a great time trying to figure out what in the world it means. It has something to do with how the people were able to determine what God wanted them to know. And though it is not clear to us, I can assure you it was perfectly clear to the Israelites. They knew this was the way in which God's mind could be known. So you see, they are really without excuse at this point. There

95

was a means to find out what the mind of the Lord was—but they did not use that means.

There is a way in which you can find out God's purposes for your life today: It is found in Scripture; it is found in the leading of the Holy Spirit; it is found in the ways in which people of God can advise you; it is found in the providential acts of God. Put them all together and I think you can know the will of God. But the problem with so many of us is that we rush ahead. There may be a time when we ought to pause and wait—as it relates to a marriage, a job or any decision. Find out! God will let you know. Do not just walk by sight. Exercise faith! Do not just confide in your own wisdom or rely on your own judgment. Seek the Lord in everything, for Scripture says, "In everything, by prayer and petition . . . present your requests to God" (Phil. 4:6).

God's people disregarded counsel and consequently that put them in a bad spot.

Deliverance Through God's Mercy

Finally, there was a deliverance through God's mercy. The Gibeonites made this pact with Israel through deceit and the upshot of it was that they became hewers of wood and carriers of water. They became the servants. They had to do the menial tasks. But notice! Their lives were spared. There was deliverance here, both for the Israelites and for the Gibeonites.

For Israel, first of all, we can see that they were able to understand that God can turn the wrath of men into praise for Him. God overrules for the benefit of His people. God can turn our mistakes into advantages. That is the mercy and the greatness of the Lord. Do not presume on it, but the principle is here. God, in His mercy, turned a dreadful mistake into a blessing. He has done that for us again and again, has He not? We can trust Him in that direction.

The other side of the coin has to do with the Gibeonites. As a punishment they became the slaves of the people of God. But this benefited them, too. They lived! They became the objects of the mercy of God, and life went on. Not in the same direction, but it did go on. They were not ruined.

Sometimes people say, "Oh, that past of mine, that dreadful mistake I made, that awful step I took in the wrong direction—it's ruined my life forever." But God gives grace that we might serve Him. Even if you have made a mistake, there is hope for you. You owe your life to God's mercy. Serve Him, then, with gladness.

The Gibeonites are a good illustration of how God gives us grace so that we might serve Him. They had a specific job to do all the days of their lives which put them in touch with God. It put them in close proximity to His Tabernacle. It kept them in touch with His people. It was God's mercy being expressed again and again. I used to think they ended up as nothing but slaves. Now I have discovered, even in this difficult and sinful situation, God's mercy was exercised and there was hope for them. They took a new lease on life and they moved from where they were.

There are some things, my friend, about which you can do nothing so far as the past is concerned, beyond asking God's forgiveness. When you have the assurance, according to His Word, that He has forgiven you, start at *that point* and move on as a servant of God, the kind of person whom God can bless and use for His glory. I find great encouragement in that, and I hope you do as well.

The Gibeonites were not just woodchoppers and water carriers. Oh, they were that, but they had the opportunity of recognizing that because of the mercy of God there was hope and new vision and new experience, and God met them where they were. God will meet you where you are, and in His mercy and grace give you opportunity for service and for fellowship.

8
Guilty as Charged

Joshua 10, 11

Chapter 10 is full of great energy and action. In fact, action verbs spring out at us everywhere as we read the story.

The surrounding communities heard of the success of Joshua and his armies. They knew that God was not on their side but was with the Israelites. They knew that, unless some remarkable change of events took place, they were directly in line for attack and battle with Joshua and his remarkable armies. Thus, one of the kings realized that if they were to survive, all five of the kings would have to form an alliance. So the man who is known as the King of Jerusalem sent out a call to the towns of Hebron, Jarmuth, Lachish and Eglon. These were all towns within a few miles and it was perfectly natural that they should attempt to align themselves against what they considered to be their common enemy.

These five kings rallied and sent out their combined armies against Gibeon. The intelligence forces of Gibeon heard of the approaching danger and the decision from that city was to send out a call for help to Gilgal where Joshua was residing. The call included a strong reminder of the treaty that had been made between Gilgal and Joshua.

Now look at verse 8. "The Lord said to Joshua, 'Do not be afraid of them; I have given them into your hand. Not one of them will be able to withstand you.'" Here is a remarkable fresh promise from the Lord that Joshua needed just at this time. God was faithful to supply him with assurance and direction. As a result, Joshua immediately went after the enemies and engaged in that strange battle during which the daylight was prolonged, hailstones fell from heaven and an overwhelming victory was afforded the Israelites.

One of the first things that strikes us as we read on is the element of fear. There was the fear of those who rejected God. They sensed that someone divine was behind the remarkable victories of Joshua. Fear of this kind always seems to lead to action that tends to produce further grounds for more fear. They failed to turn to the things of the Lord and thus they moved inexorably down the pathway that led to great difficulty.

Then there was the fear of Gibeon. These people recently formed a league with Joshua. They entered into a treaty and now they were calling upon that for fulfillment. We can see here how important it is to get on the right side. It is essential that we be on God's side. The more we get to know God and His ways, the less afraid we will find ourselves.

Then, for Joshua, there was the strong assurance, "Do not be afraid!" The assurance that was Joshua's was based on his position as well as upon his experience. There is a hard lesson involved in this matter. It involves the tension of utter trust and the resultant peace, against the need for work and valiant effort. Joshua was dependent upon God, yet there was much for him to do as leader of the army. God promised that He was going to do certain great and mighty things, yet Joshua had the responsibility. So this speaks to our own situation today.

In the context of this chapter, then, we see the need of Gibeon, the faithfulness of Joshua and the help of God. Then comes the great story of the miracle of the sun standing still. People have a fascinating time trying to explain this and understand it. Certainly it was a miracle. Whether is was brought about by refraction, a shifting of the earth's axis or by some other means, we are not sure. We do know that light was extended until God's purposes were accomplished, and the timing and the resultant activity were miraculous.

Now, that gives us the background for three things we need to review at this time. These are principles to encourage and strengthen us in our own Christian living today.

God Is at Work

What a joy it is to see the Lord's hand of power and blessing all around the world. For instance, God is at work in Asia. There is tremendous response to the gospel in many places in that part of the world. In Korea, the Church is increasing many times faster than the population. In certain places of northeastern India, Christians actually make up a majority of the population and thus are able to affect the entire social structure of that part of the land.

In Latin America, people are responding in unprecedented numbers to the work of the gospel. Thousands upon thousands of people are turning to the Saviour. In North America there also are fascinating things taking place, especially among our youth. We mention all of this to simply point out that, indeed, God is at work in the world today, even as He was in Joshua's time, so long ago.

However, there are also obstacles! Everything is not rosy! We must never forget that we wrestle not against flesh and blood, but against principalities and spiritual wickedness in high places (see Eph. 6:12). We must recognize that when there is great blessing, there is also increased resistance. For example, on a trip through certain segments of Africa not too long ago, I was informed that the response to the gospel in that particular place was very limited. In fact, we have more members in Park Street Church here in Boston than Christians in some whole segments of the continent of Africa. On the other hand, the prediction is that by the end of this century, because of the remarkable response in so many places within those nations, Africa could be substantially Christian.

What will come of all of this activity? What is God doing in the world today? We cannot be certain, of course, but let us remember that out of the evangelical awakening in the early eighteenth century came the whole modern missionary movement. There does seem to be a great sweep of God's Spirit today. We have talked to a great many people as we have traveled around the world and a large percentage of those people are professing Christians. God is at work, and for this we are deeply grateful.

There Is Much Yet to Be Done

Someone has referred to this as the age of the evangelical. Polls seems to indicate that there are millions upon millions of professing evangelicals in America. Politicians are wondering how this potential force can be harnessed to their own use. Church leaders are reviewing this great mass of people with a new sense of respect and wonderment. The secular world is increasingly aware of this segment of society. This indeed may be the age for the evangelical and surely it is our responsibility to move while the opportunity is before us.

As one who has been deeply interested in the ministry and work of the National Association of Evangelicals, I have been asking as many questions as I can and constantly seeking answers to the ways and means by which unitedly we may press forward in the light of these great opportunities. Oftentimes the single answer that comes back to me is, "Get the churches involved in outreach." Surely we need to take advantage of this evangelistic mood of our day.

What a remarkable thing would take place if the growth rate of 10,000 churches in America could be substantially increased. This would create a wave that would make its impact felt all across our land.

Evangelism is the word for our day. Of course it always has been but it seems to have special significance and implication at this particular time. Evangelism is that which confronts people with the claims of the Lord Jesus Christ. This can be done through the radio, the printed page, new missionary endeavor and much effort. Great conferences can be held, excellent speeches and seminars can be offered, wonderful training programs can be presented. But in the final analysis, we must not drift back to our own ways of doing things, but rather we must seek God's plan for genuine evangelism.

What new goals do we have before us? Could not

every church in America, regardless of its size, set some specific goals and move toward those goals in terms of new people for the Lord? Of course we recognize that conversion is God's business. Certainly our dependence is upon the ministry of the Holy Spirit. But we need to be studying these remarkable happenings and attempting to get handles upon them so that we may grasp them and move forward together. Great study is going on in churches and in institutions all across the world. New committees are being formed in many local churches. New emphases are being given from the pulpits. New opportunities for training are afforded by many congregations. A tremendous emphasis is being given to the whole matter of church growth and its great possibilities.

Let us look at church growth for just a moment. Sometimes people involved in church growth efforts have been accused of moving away from dependency upon the Holy Spirit. If that is true, then of course such church growth efforts need to be warned against and condemned. Certainly our only hope is in the grace and the power of God's Spirit as He ministers and convicts. We are not in a numbers game in the Christian Church. Our responsibility is not simply to be able to point with some degree of pride to 1,000, 100 or 10 new members in a given situation. We need to review the attitudes that are ours within our own churches.

Some churches do not want to grow and are quite content to stay small and thus seemingly secure. It is not easy to assimilate new people into this kind of situation. Change always brings with it certain adjustments and many times we are resistant to this. But the fact remains, we are under the obligation of going into all the world and preaching the gospel, and that means beginning in our own immediate area. Evangelism must be the basic concern of every congregation and of every Christian. Evangelism, missionary endeavor and outreach is not an option that can be voted upon when a congregation feels like it. It is not something that can be taken as an extracurricular type of thing, such as a course in school. Evangelism is the heart of worship and service to God.

We need to keep in mind that programs can oftentimes divert us from our basic concern. To simply pick up a program from some other church and try to impose it upon our situation may or may not work. We cannot always copy what someone else has done and expect it to work. I remember reading an amazingly involved proclamation on the label on a bottle of medicine that was concocted many, many years ago. It listed all that the remedy could do for an individual. Sometimes programs of evangelism are suggested in this same light. We must not be guilty of trusting in an oversimplification, but we must want to grow.

The School of World Missions at Fuller Theological Seminary in California suggests in much of its material that there is need for *internal growth*. That is, there must be church renewal, emphasis upon prayer, renewed devotion to Christ and to each other and a fresh understanding and vision of the Lord's work. We need this and should earnestly pray for it. In addition, there is need for *expansive growth*. This simply means, as I understand it, the adding of membership to the rolls of the church. There must be that kind of growth as evidence of the activity of the spread of the gospel in our community.

Also, there could well be the growth of *extension*. This would involve the beginnings of new churches in new communities or new places where the witness is not what it should be. Finally, there is what that church growth mate-

105

rial refers to as *bridging growth*. This would involve reaching out into other cultures, or the missionary emphasis that needs to spring from the church. These all point out that evangelism and growth are part of God's purpose for His people. We must be aware of that which He is doing and then also be aware of the fact that there is much yet to be done.

Let God Do It

Finally, there is the great asssurance that God will sustain us in all of this. The miracle that we see in Joshua came as an answer to prayer. God said to Joshua that he was not to be afraid. Joshua was uncertain as to the direction in which he should go until he got clear indication from the Lord, and then he pressed on. As you will read in chapter 10, verse 14, "There has never been a day like it before or since, a day when the LORD listened to a man. Surely the LORD was fighting for Israel!" Joshua's pleas unto God resulted in power from God. Prayer causes weak men to become strong, speechless men to be able to speak with authority and power and sinful men to turn to the Lord Jesus Christ for salvation.

We need God's power in order to do God's work. We need to be Spirit-led and Spirit-filled people. We must faithfully proclaim the good news of the gospel and trust God to speak to people. This is His work. It can only be done in His way and for His glory. We must respond to the challenge, even as Joshua did in his day.

The obstacles may loom large. We may look upon our experience in the past and wonder how it would be possible for us to accomplish the large order which God has given us. But it can be done! It is being done! God will continue to undergird the efforts of His people as we cast ourselves upon His mercy and as we earnestly seek to do His will. And as Joshua was wonderfully encouraged of the Lord in the past, so let us rise to the task of evangelism and missionary outreach today.

The Christian's Battles

The kings of the north were worried. They got together at a place called Merom, west and north of the Sea of Galilee, and there they formed an alliance. The Jewish historian Josephus estimated that there were at least 300,000 armed footmen, 10,000 horsemen and 20,000 chariots in the army of this alliance. His figures may or may not be accurate, but we can be sure that this was the largest army and the greatest opposition Israel had yet faced.

What can we learn from this part of Israel's history? Paul the apostle said, "For everything that was written in the past was written to teach us, so that through endurance and the encouragement of the Scripures we might have hope" (Rom. 15:4). As we look at Joshua and the Israelites, we find that they had to go through many trials before they gained the Promised Land.

Christians today face many battles, too.

Over and over in Scripture the Christian life is likened to warfare. There are places in the Bible that suggest there are enemies which war against the soul. There is warfare between right and wrong—between God and Satan. There is a spiritual struggle and there is also the assurance of divine protection and ultimate victory.

Paul described his experience of being at war within himself. "For what I do is not the good I want to do; no, the evil I do not want to do—this I keep on doing" (Rom. 7:19). He went on, "But I see another law at work in the

107

members of my body, waging war against the law of my mind and making me a prisoner of the law" (Rom. 7:23). Another time he wrote, "For though we live in the world, we do not wage war as the world does. The weapons we fight with are not the weapons of the world. On the contrary, they have divine power to demolish strongholds. We demolish arguments and every pretension that sets itself up against the knowledge of God, and we take captive every thought to make it obedient to Christ" (2 Cor. 10:3-5).

To Timothy, Paul wrote, "So that by following them you may fight the good fight" (1 Tim. 1:18). Another time he wrote, "Endure hardship with us like a good soldier of Christ Jesus" (2 Tim. 2:3).

So the New Testament suggests the analogy of the Christian engaged in a battle. When we turn to the Old Testament we see the people of God having to work their way by battle, effort and strong endurance against an enemy who is resisting them every step of the way, until finally they come to the Promised Land. We can pick up that picture and put it alongside the New Testament idea, and it will help us understand our own battles in our service to God.

Believers are given weapons and armor for fighting the battles (see Eph. 6:11-17). In the Old Testament, God is often pictured as a conqueror, shield or a fortress, as one who stands for the defenseless. The Christian life is a battle, and we are expected to fight the good fight (see 1 Tim. 6:12). We are taught to appreciate the strength of the enemy, to lean on God's power and to operate under His authority. Toil, strain, suffering, exposure to danger, all characterize the life-style of the Christian. The highest ambition of the Christian is to "please his commanding officer" (2 Tim. 2:4). That's the challenge God puts before us, for we are indeed in a conflict.

In this conflict we can learn another lesson from Joshua. Back in chapter 10, five enemy kings fled from the battle and hid in a cave. Joshua had some men block up the mouth of the cave and guard it while the rest of the troops finished off the rest of the enemy. Now you might think that in the heat of the battle Joshua would forget all about those five kings in the cave, or that he would decide to spare their lives. But Joshua brought them out and disposed of them. They represented the enemy and had to be done away with. They were destroyed before the people of God left the area for further conquests.

I think there is a principle to be learned here: leave nothing of the old behind that will someday rise up and haunt you. The old nature, with which we were born into this world, is always there. It is not possible for that nature to produce anything that is holy. It can produce a lot of other things, some very generous and eloquent things. But it can never produce anything that God can look upon as holy. In contrast to that, Scripture teaches us that there is a new nature. That new nature comes by our faith in Christ; the new nature cannot sin because it is of God Himself. Our battle involves the crucifixion of the old self which remains with us and opposes our new nature.

If we are to have a victorious Christian life, sin cannot be left lurking in the caves. The Word of God clearly teaches us that we are to get rid of it. We do that by confessing it to God, by forsaking that sin, by condemning it.

Winning this battle is never easy. You think you've done away with a certain sin once and for all. Then you let your guard down for half a second and it's there. You think you've won a certain battle and that you will never again have to step out into that field of conflict; then you turn around and it's back again. Even though that old nature of ours is just beneath the surface, we cannot excuse our actions that are sinful and wrong just because we are human. We excuse ourselves again and again; we say, "Well, what do you expect, I'm human, that's my weakness." But the Bible says we are to be superhuman. Not through superhuman efforts, but because of that new nature that resides within us. "For sin shall not be your master" (Rom. 6:14). God's power is available to us in our battles.

Christians should be so sensitive to the things that are wrong and displeasing to God that we shy away from them and ask God's Spirit to preserve and protect us. Christian is our name, Jesus is our Saviour and our responsibility is to live accordingly. You belong to God and Jesus Christ, and thus your life is no longer to be ruled by temper. Your life is no longer to be ruled by that loose tongue that can cut people down in a minute. Your life is no longer to be ruled by that overwhelming temptation that has hounded you and belabored you for years. You are a Christian. The Holy Spirit of God lives within you, and you ought to be engaged in a conflict, fighting against sin.

Joshua's secret in war or anything else was his obedience. We must obey in the same way. We must obey the same God. He's on the side of those who will trust Him.

The Christian's Conduct

We are to live in conduct that befits our Christianity. The Christian is to exercise true faith. We must constantly rely on unseen help. Look at the development of faith in the book of Joshua. At Jericho, God manifested Himself in dramatic and thunderous ways and the walls came tumbling down. No question about who intervened there. God was not quite so manifest at Ai; He was less visible, but His promises were as sure. At Beth-horon God extended the day and sent the hail. That was a major battle; but in the smaller battles, these people were learning to walk by faith and not by sight.

Can we learn that same thing? Can we learn to endure as seeing Him who is invisible? True faith believes when little can be seen. God tries His people gradually. He will not allow us to be tempted above what we can bear (see 1 Cor. 10:13). God cultivates that faith in your heart and mine. He says, as He said to Joshua again and again, "Don't be afraid, I will deliver you." Oh! that we could learn to live in the light of those promises and exercise that faith. It is a battle; it is difficult, but that is God's standard of conduct for His people.

That standard of conduct requires that the Christian be a servant. "My servant Joshua"; "My servant Moses." We often seem to forget the servant aspect of our conduct. Jesus set the pattern: He emptied Himself, He took upon Himself the form of a servant and He humbled Himself. He became obedient and died as part of that obedience (see Phil. 2:7,8). Mark tells us that Jesus came not to be served but to serve (see Mark 10:45). His suffering was predicted by Isaiah, who said He would be "despised and rejected by men" (Isa. 53:3). Those of us who believe in this suffering Servant are to serve.

Does our conduct bear the mark of servanthood? Do we make our decisions in the light of the fact that we are to serve God? Do we find it possible to justify our actions and our purposes and our ambitions to the suffering Servant? That really is what we have to do. You do not have to justify those things to your pastor or to your church. But as a believer in the Lord Jesus Christ you must consider in the light of justification to the suffering Servant every detail of your life and every decision you make.

And what about our leadership? We hear a great deal about that. We go to seminars and learn how to be leaders. We buy books to learn how to be leaders. We do not lead just because we are loud. Our authority in our leadership lies in our serving. That is what Jesus said.

Our conduct involves servanthood; our conduct also requires that the Christian resist the tug of the world. Have you thought about that in terms of the conquest that was going on in the Promised Land? The conflict was not all on the battlefield. Part of it, I am sure, was the temptation to enjoy the good life that was available in Palestine. "Joshua, let's knock off all this scrapping. Let's quit all this battle stuff and let's settle down and enjoy ourselves for a while." That shouldn't be hard for us to identify with because that is exactly the kind of temptation under which we live day by day. The Church must be different. Let us never forget the radicalness of Jesus' call.

9
Give Me This Mountain!

Joshua 13, 18

What do you think of when you hear the word *inheritance*? You might think of money, land, furniture or some valuable object that someone may leave you. Sometimes we inherit things that are not so pleasant. A new administration in the government usually inherits a few problems from the former administration. Sometimes people complain about the personality traits they feel they have inherited from their ancestors. Inheritance can mean many things.

We have come to the point in the book of Joshua where the tribes begin receiving their inheritance in the Promised Land. Chapter 12 recapitulated the taking of the land, battle by battle. The land is pretty well subdued, from Kadesh in the extreme south to Mount Hermon in the north. The east side of the Jordan was Israel's, as well as of the land on the west.

Promise of Inheritance

Joshua is now an old man according to chapter 13, and there is much yet to be accomplished. God instructs Joshua concerning the division of the land, telling him what portion each tribe should have. The people have fought well and bravely and God has honored their commitment to Himself and His purposes. Just as He promised many generations before, the land is now theirs. This is their inheritance.

There are almost 100 references in the Bible that have to do with the matter of inheritance. Canaan was the inheritance of the people of God. The Levites, instead of land, had God Himself for their inheritance (see Josh. 13:33). The nation Israel was looked upon as Jehovah's inheritance (see Ps. 33:12).

The messianic King is to receive the nations for an inheritance. And God's promises are seen as an inheritance that belongs to His people.

In the figurative or poetic sense, the expression applies basically to the Kingdom of God becoming an inheritance for the people of God. But the spiritualizing of the concept is not left to the New Testament alone; it can be found also in the Old Testament. The first promise of the inheritance of the people of God was to Abraham and to his descendants. The possession of this inheritance rested solely on the gift of God. Even though it was entered into with hard fighting, it was basically God's gift. The land was to be possessed forever, but it was based on a condition: the faithfulness of the people of God.

In contrast to that conditional covenant, the New Testament presents a new covenant, a better inheritance (see Heb. 8:6-13). That inheritance is in Christ. Paul says that we are joint heirs of God with Christ (see Rom. 8:16,17).

The inheritance belongs to the Lord Jesus Christ, and it is ours by His grace. The enjoyment of God's inheritance begins now; but the full possession of God's inheritance is yet to come.

The Bible is a unity. The purpose of Scripture is to unfold the story of redemption. It traces in history and in doctrine the development of the divine purpose of God in the salvation of humanity. This theme runs through the Bible from beginning to end. That is why it is perfectly legitimate to turn to the Old Testament to find lessons and applications for people who are living under a new covenant. Because of the unity of Scripture, the historical event in Joshua 13, which is the story of the inheritance of God's people, may be used as an application to the inheritance of the people of God in our time.

Promise of Future Hope

The theme of inheritance emphasizes in part the matter of future hope. Thomas Guthrie, a Scottish preacher who lived several generations ago, wrote a very fine book entitled *Christ and the Inheritance of the Saints*. He quotes from Colossians 1:12: "Giving thanks to the Father, who has qualified you to share in the inheritance of the saints in the kingdom of light." Guthrie speaks of Jacob's dream of the ladder in Genesis 28:12-15. He says that the ladder is an emblem of the scheme of salvation, for it is the restoration of communication between God in heaven and man on earth. Jacob, in the dream, saw angels ascending and descending. This beautiful word picture brings to our attention the whole redemptive history of God![1]

It is great to know that we have as part of our inheritance the hope of heaven. The Bible describes this in no uncertain terms. It says, "The soul who sins is the one who will die" (Ezek. 18:4); that is very clear. But believers are made alive in Christ forevermore (see 1 Cor. 15:22; Rom. 6:23).

Heaven is not a reward for our hard work. The laborer earns his wages, but an inheritance is not a wage to be earned. Heaven is not attained by conquest, but by heritage. It is God's free gift. It is the fulfillment of all Jesus said He was going to do when He promised, "I will come back and take you to be with me" (John 14:3).

Promise of Present Experience

Finally, let us look at the inheritance God has given us in relationship to our present experience. We should not stop with contemplating our future joy. We need to remember that the inheritance God has made available for the saints is also reflected in our present situation. What difference does our inheritance make to us *today* as believers in the Lord Jesus Christ?

We ought to have a new knowledge of God as part of the inheritance that belongs to us. This was a goal of the apostle Paul. He said, "I want to know Christ and the power of His resurrection and the fellowship of sharing in His sufferings" (Phil. 3:10). This, I believe, comes through a new knowledge of Scripture. We need to be studying Scripture on our own and in groups as part of the inheritance of God.

We need to have a new vision—a world vision. We need to see this world, as Donald McGavran says, through church-growth eyes; through eyes that are saying, How can we see the spread of the gospel? How can we confront new communities with the good news of Christ? I believe when that new vision becomes ours, then new effort will result. The apostle Paul, in giving his testimony, said, "I worked harder than all of them" (1 Cor. 15:10). People sometimes look down their noses at hard work. But I think we would work a lot harder if we had that new vision.

Not only is there a need for a new knowledge and a new vision of God, but also there is a new power available to us. Ephesians 1:13,14 speaks of it. We have been sealed with the Holy Spirit of God, and this is the guarantee of our inheritance until the redemption of the purchased possession. It is God's goal that we be conformed to the image of His Son. In Joshua's day, God gave each tribe what He thought was best for that tribe. He does the same for us.

One can go back to the story of Abraham and Lot and very quickly see that one seemed to walk by sight and the other walked by faith. Abraham, you will recall, let God choose for him the direction in which he should go. God outlined for him that which was His purpose for Abraham's life.

We have seen all through the book of Joshua the continued unfolding of God's plan. First there was a battle, then there was the faithfulness of God and the overcoming of temptation, and now Joshua stands upon the verge of his inheritance. This unfolding of truth must make a difference in our attitudes and in our relationships.

Sometimes it is difficult to describe what is happening in our lives because it is so meaningful and it is so full of the things of the Lord. When all a Christian can say is, "Come and see," then I feel that indeed God is at work in that individual's life.

Do you sense the presence of the Lord in your present experience? The inheritance that belongs to you is an inheritance that will give you a sense of victory and assurance of the power and peace of God all the days of your life. Rejoice this day in that which God has made available to you.

Begin to Possess Your Possessions

In Joshua 18 we find the children of Israel assembling together at a place called Shiloh, which is north of the great city of Jericho. In the preceding chapters, we read that the Israelites started dividing up the land. The tribe of Judah got the land in the south. Joseph was assigned the center portion of the land. Then apparently for some reason there was a pause or a delay in the division. Here in chapter 18 they get started again.

Shiloh is up the Jordan Valley and northwest of Gilgal. It is just about the center of the land. Interestingly enough, the name *Shiloh* means rest, and it is an indication of something God was going to do for His people. The town of Shiloh would be the site of the Tabernacle of the people of God for the next 300 years, until the time of Samuel.

When Saul came on the scene, the Tabernacle was moved to a place called Nob; during King David's reign it was moved to a place called Gibeon. Finally it was permanently settled, no longer as the Tabernacle, but as the Temple, which Solomon constructed in the city of Jerusalem.

Here at Shiloh, Joshua had to prod the Israelites to get on with the job, "How long will you wait before you begin to take possession of the land that the Lord . . . has given you?" (Josh. 18:3). Maybe you have heard sermons that challenge Christian people to possess their possessions; that's the emphasis I see in this story. We are charged by God to possess those things which belong to us.

118

For a Particular Group Only

Note that these possessions are only for a particular group of people—those who have put faith in Jesus Christ. This is stressed many times in the Bible.

The word *Shiloh* is also used in Genesis 49:10 *(KJV):* "The sceptre shall not depart from Judah, nor a lawgiver from between his feet, until Shiloh come." Jewish and Christian interpreters generally agree that in this verse the coming of Shiloh is apparently a reference to the Messiah.

It is interesting to notice that the expectation of a personal Saviour did not begin with Moses or with Joshua or David, but was contained in that germ of the promise way back in Genesis 3:15. It was also found in the blessing of Noah; it was further expounded in the promises of God to the patriarchs.

Jacob, in blessing his 12 sons, indicated that through his fourth son, Judah, would come the Messiah. Judah would bear the sceptre with lion-like courage until Shiloh would come (see Gen. 49:9,10). The tribe of Judah led in the battle after the death of Joshua (see Judg. 1:1,2). From Judah came the first judge (see Judg. 3:9,10; Num. 13:6). From this tribe came David and Solomon. Isaiah spoke of the Prince of Peace as a distinct reference to Christ (see Isa. 9:6). The Lion of the tribe of Judah in Revelation 5:5 is the Lord Jesus Christ.

Christ is the King of kings, and it is only by faith in Him that we have the ability to possess the possessions that belong to the people of God; only because of the covenant relationship by which we belong to His family; only to believers in the Lord Jesus Christ do the possessions belong.

Land to Be Possessed

For the Christian there is land to be possessed. Joshua asked the people, "How long are you going to wait? That land is available; the possession has been made available; it is yours." Two tribes had possessed their possessions but the others had not.

Have we possessed what God has made available for us? Are we satisfied as Christians with where we are, with the place in which we reside? Have we received only a portion? Have we only stepped inside the door when God wants us to enter into all the rooms He has prepared for us?

Are we content to stay only on familiar ground in the Bible—the great chapters? Many people in their quiet times turn to the great chapters of the Bible and find encouragement and blessing and help from them. There is nothing wrong with this, but we should also press on, "Therefore let us leave the elementary teachings about Christ and go on to maturity" (Heb. 6:1). Let us now leave the first principles of Christ, not to turn our backs on them by any means, but to build on them and to move on to new relationships, new understanding and new growth in the things of the Lord.

There is a call in the Bible for well-rounded, stable, balanced, growing Christians. That applies to us all. People these days are experts, specialists. But Christians have no business being such specialists that they neglect some parts of their Christian growth. When a well-rounded, glowing, stable Christian becomes aware of a lack in his life, he begins to work on it; he asks God to help him. No single spiritual characteristic is to be exercised at the expense of other Christian principles.

One area of "possessions" Christian people should

consider is that of spiritual gifts. Scripture says: "If anyone speaks, he should do it as one speaking the very words of God. If anyone serves, he should do it with the strength God provides" (1 Pet. 4:11). I think that verse identifies two general areas of spiritual gifts: the speaking area and the serving area. (Some people think there is a third category, the signifying, or supernatural gifts. But I feel that all of the gifts can be grouped in the two categories of speaking and serving.)

There is great misunderstanding about spiritual gifts. Some Christian people do very little in the Lord's service; when challenged on it, they respond, "I can't. This is not something for me to get involved in, because I just don't have any spiritual gifts." However, other people are doing so many things, working so hard in the church and for the things of the Lord, they seem to have no time for the things they perhaps ought to be doing.

This is one of the tensions in the church: some people do not do anything; some people have to do it all. We need to help each other discover our spiritual gifts. I believe those spiritual gifts are often simply the turn of personality and the obvious qualities in our makeup.

Ephesians 4:7 says, "But to each one of us grace has been given as Christ has apportioned it." And 1 Corinthians 12:7 says, "Now to each one the manifestation of the Spirit is given for the common good." Paul goes on to list some of the gifts; then he says, "All these are the work of one and the same Spirit, and he gives them to each one, just as he determines" (v. 11). It would seem then that every Christian has been given one or more gifts. We need to discover them; for surely when we talk about possessing our possessions, we must be concerned with the gifts God has given each one of us, personally.

121

Some people seem to have so many gifts. Some of our missionaries, for example, seem to be able to do anything. But often that is because they *have* to. Maybe one of the reasons we haven't discovered much about our spiritual gifts is that we have not been forced to make use of those gifts. Missionaries do not have the pleasure of leaning back and saying, "Let somebody else do it," because there is nobody else to do it.

I suggest, then, that we get busy. For even apart from our particular gift or gifts, we are all instructed in Scripture to evangelize, exhort, show mercy and help. And as we obey, the Holy Spirit often shows us gifts we did not know we had. Such gifts usually take time to develop. God often incorporates our gifts in our inclinations. Discover your gifts and cultivate them for God.

Other people may sometimes be very helpful in encouraging you to discover your gifts. But I do not believe others should be the final word as to whether or not we have particular gifts. G. Campbell Morgan became one of the greatest expository preachers of his generation. But the first time he applied as a candidate for the ministry he was rejected and told he was not ministerial material. But Morgan was convinced, in spite of what others had to say, including his close friends and well-meaning supporters, that God led him into the ministry. He said, "I am going to be a minister," and indeed he did become just that.

God ought to be the final word. I do not mean to say that God does not use friends and encouragement, for He may do so. But God is the final word.

There is no room for pride in our gift, no matter what it may be (see 1 Cor. 4:7). We are warned, also, not to idolize those who do have a gift (see 1 Cor. 3:3-7).

Be content with God's choice of gifts for you. Do not feel guilty or envious if somebody else has different gifts. Gifts help us toward maturity. The apostle Peter said that each of us should use whatever spiritual gifts he has received in order to serve others (see 1 Pet. 4:10). We are to possess our possessions, and part of those possessions lie in the direction of the spiritual gifts God has made available to His own.

Finally, all of the above is based on faith and confidence in the promises of the Lord. In our study we have seen that our ability to possess our possessions is based on faith in Christ, illustrated in the text by the land to be possessed on the part of God's people. Now we will show that understanding all of this is based on faith.

Joshua tells about the time, 45 years before, that he and several others were chosen by Moses to spy out the Promised Land. All the spies except two returned with a report that "made the hearts of the people melt with fear" (Josh. 14:8). Only two, Caleb and Joshua, saw the *possibilities* of God! We are never to give up on that. That vision, that confidence will carry you for 45 years, or whatever period of time is needed. Joshua's eye remained undimmed and his vision remained clear all through those years. He carried that goal before him.

Thus, this faith is our own possession today. Faith in the Lord Jesus Christ and His promises will overcome the giants in the land of our own hearts. In Numbers 14:24 we read, "But because my servant Caleb has a different spirit and follows me wholeheartedly, I will bring him into the land he went to, and his descendants will inherit it." Caleb knew that God would be faithful. And this faithfulness of God remains one of our great possessions today. Not one word of anything God promised has failed. He cannot fail. He will do what He says He will do.

Our responsibility today then is to catch a vision of the Lord Jesus Christ. That vision will sustain you in your youth; that vision will sustain you in trouble, old age and death. Look ahead to the Lamb of God. You will never need to look back.

Footnote

1. Thomas Guthrie, *Christ and the Inheritance of the Saints* (Grand Rapids: Zondervan Publishing House, n.d.), p. 1.

10
God, Our Refuge

Joshua 20, 21

Remember the song lyrics, "When Johnny comes marching home again hurrah, hurrah"? What happens then? Many things. You may have had that experience yourself. You have come back from service and found a new life and a new way of doing things. You used the benefits of the G.I. bill to go to school. Or you bought a home or found a new career. But eventually, routine sets in.

This is true also in the Christian life. The Christian life is a battle and the battle is never over. In that sense, then, Johnny the Christian will not come marching home from the Christian battles. These battles do not end. But routine is nevertheless part of our experience. The Christian life is marked by routine, just as anyone's. Routine is with us, but it need not be dull.

Here in Joshua we find a new phase in the experience of the people of God. "When they had finished dividing the land into its allotted portions, the Israelites gave Joshua an inheritance among them . . . . These are the territories that Eleazar the priest, Joshua the son of Nun . . .

125

assigned . . . . And so they finished dividing the land" (Josh. 19:49,51). They battled to win the land; now they entered into a new phase of distributing the land.

We see a whole new way of life stretching out before the people of God. Seven years of fighting are behind them. They can look back on the crossing of the Jordan, the conquest of Jericho and many other experiences of God's power. The enemy is subdued; the land is divided. Now it is time to get back to farming and to grazing the herds and the flocks. Routine.

We in the Christian life will continue to face many crises. But we need to learn how to cope with the routine activities of life—how to live victoriously in the midst of those routine activities and not just muddle our way through.

People discover when they go to the mission field, for example, that their activities are not all centered in public meetings, preaching and Bible classes. They find there is a great deal of ordinary, sometimes grinding, routine activity that must be done. Missionaries learn, as all people of God learn as they serve Him, that it is essential to translate decision and great feeling, and great emotion, into daily living and the service to God.

It is all too easy for believers to spend time wandering in the desert rather than enjoying the land God has made available. He has provided it for all of us. The secret to enjoying what God has made available is found in one word: *obedience*—obedience to the command of God. The secret of possessing our possessions is directly related to our willingness to do what God would have us do. Not only can we possess the land, but in the routine, day-to-day activities, we can find fulfillment and enjoyment. It is a resource that God has made available to His people, but it

126

must be utilized if it is going to count for anything.

Dr. Alan Redpath tells a story that illustrates this. Many years ago the English and the Scots were fighting against each other. In a certain place in England, which you can still see today, there were a number of different castle towers. They were apparently fortifications where people could defend themselves and be ready for action against the enemy. The English were in these castles and towers, and the Scots began to lay siege against them.

Some of the towers had their water supply piped in. As soon as the Scots discovered this, they severed the pipelines. That shut off the water and soon the English were no longer able to defend the castles. But other towers had been built in a close relationship to springs of water from which the people could draw their resources; these proved invulnerable.[1]

I think this is a marvelous illustration of the very thing we are talking about here. If we, in our Christian life, must look to the outside for the sustaining graces and for the encouragement that will keep us on an even keel, we are going to be in trouble. If we are dependent upon circumstances, conditions and people who are outside, those things will fail. And then we will fail too. But if, like the tower that is built over the spring, you have *inner* resources, you too will be invulnerable.

Cities of Refuge

Now let us see what happened in some of the routine activities once Israel had taken the land. First, we will take a look at the cities of refuge as described in chapter 20. God instructed the people to establish six cities of refuge, three on each side of the Jordan.

Such a provision was needed because of the culture of

the day. If a person was killed, another member of the family would take it upon himself to hunt down and kill the one responsible. This vengeance wiped out the chance for a proper trial and occasionally resulted in the death of innocent persons. So God, in His mercy, provided these cities of refuge to protect the one who had unintentionally killed another.

Deuteronomy 19 also discusses the cities of refuge. They were not havens for all kinds of wicked people, as some of the temple areas of the ancient world proved to be. They were established for the limited purpose of protecting one type of person, that one who accidentally killed another.

The city of refuge is a word picture of something we can apply to our lives today. It is a picture of our Lord Jesus Christ. The only place where you can find forgiveness, the only place where you can go to be set free, is in the person of our Lord Jesus Christ. He becomes for us a city of refuge. He is our great High Priest. In Him is the source of our salvation. Psalm 143:9 says, "Rescue me from my enemies, O Lord, for I hide myself in you." Hebrews 6:18 speaks of those "who have fled to take hold of the hope offered to us." And Paul, in Philippians 3:9 expresses a desire to "Be found in him, not having a righteousness of my own that comes from the law, but that which is through faith in Christ."

Picture an accident that results in the death of another person. This would be a dreadful thing, as you can appreciate. There lies the victim. His death was unintentional but his family as well as the rest of the community are in an uproar. What does this one do who has caused the death? All of his routine has been shattered. "Where shall I go?" says this man; "How shall I escape?"

There is an analogy here. When the sinner is awakened to his condition and begins to realize that he stands under the judgment of God, he asks the same thing. "What must I do? Where can I go?" The City of Refuge is there for you as you turn and accept what Christ has done for you. You must flee to it. Deuteronomy 19:5 says, "That man may flee to one of these cities and save his life."

Tradition in Jewish writing says that one day in every year people were sent out to repair the roads and to clear the stones and to see that the signposts that pointed to the city of refuge were legible. Part of our job today is to make the way of salvation known clearly to all the world. That is our task—to point the way clearly to the refuge afforded by Jesus Christ.

Footnote

1. Alan Redpath, *Victorious Christian Living* (Old Tappan: Fleming H. Revell Company, 1955). pp. 220, 221.

11
Caring Enough to Confront

Joshua 22

The second thing to notice, as the Israelites get settled, is the problem of false conclusions. The two-and-a-half tribes, Reuben, Gad and half of the tribe of Manasseh, staked a claim to live on the other side of the Jordan River. Moses and his successor, Joshua, approved of their claim on the condition that the fighting men of the two-and-a-half tribes must go with the rest of Israel across the river to help subdue the land. When it was all under control, they could then return to their families and to their homes (see Josh. 1:12-16).

This plan worked out fine. The tribes were loyal to the task. The fighting men were away from home for seven years, fighting for possession of the land for all Israel. Finally the land was conquered, and Joshua sent home the soldiers of Reuben, Gad and half of Manasseh.

When the people got to the edge of the Jordan River, suddenly somebody said, "Wait a minute. I see some problems here. Suppose after we go back, sometime in the future, someone should say, 'You can't really be God's people—you're on the wrong side of the river!'" And so, in order to safeguard their future connection with the rest of God's people, they decided to build a monument. They built an altar there. It looked like the altars that had been used before by the people of God for worship and sacrifice. But it was never intended for that. Their motives were pure. They simply felt they must have some kind of a monument so that, when people asked about their connection with God's people, they would have a witness. Then they could say, "There stands the altar, which is a monument. It tells the story. We fought for seven years; we fulfilled our obligation to our people; then we came home."

When the rest of the people of God heard about this altar, they jumped to a false conclusion. They thought the altar must have been put up for worship and sacrifice, and that these people on the other side of the river were no longer worshiping God. So they organized a posse.

"When the Israelites heard that they had built the altar . . . the whole assembly of Israel gathered at Shiloh, to go to war against them" (Josh. 22:11-12). They were going to go to war against their brothers. But first they sent Phinehas, the son of Eleazer the priest, and 10 leaders to check things out. This is one time that I can see justification for appointing a committee.

So Phinehas and his committee went out and accused the two-and-a-half tribes. They warned the people east of Jordan that war was coming. But the people answered them properly. They showed that their motives were sincere. This was not the first time they had been misjudged; Moses was concerned about them when they first asked for land on the east of Jordan (see Num. 32:6). But both times they straightened out the problems.

131

Have you ever witnessed a misunderstanding within the family of God? This is the people of God against the people of God. How easily a misunderstanding can occur and how damaging the results! How quickly we impute the wrong motives and how quickly this leads to civil war? That is what nearly happened to the Israelites. They had been fighting the enemy for seven years, and now they were about to fight each other.

We are quick to think the worst, to repeat what we hear and to exaggerate. We often put the worst interpretation on the actions of our fellow Christians. We fail to seek ways to understand.

There has entered into the Church across America and perhaps around the world a renewed emphasis upon the Body of Christ. We are all members of that Body. Not just a group of us. Not just those of us who have an understanding in a certain direction. But according to the Word of God we are all members of the Body. This is a great biblical truth. We need to appropriate it in the proper kind of relationship in the total Body of Christ.

If you have been misunderstood or suffered some kind of unjust treatment, you are suffering. But let me suggest that you could also be growing. You can be developing under that experience. What you do with criticism and unjust treatment is a mark of your spiritual development. Under unjust treatment, if you are not growing, I have a fearful feeling that you may be shriveling. That is dangerous.

Let us learn to be less harsh in our judgment, even if the grounds for harshness are there. Let us deal as gently as possible with the one who falls out of fellowship with the Body. Help restore that one in a spirit of meekness (see Gal. 6:1).

Praise His Name

Finally, take a look at Joshua 22:33: "They were glad to hear the report and praised God." Open strife and conflict were avoided and praise went up to God. That is what I believe ought to mark the Christian Church and the people of God. We need the ability not to jump to false conclusions and the ability to understand. When we make an attempt to work things out, civil war is pushed aside and praise goes up to God. The world has to see that. And that is a challenge and an encouragement for us in a life that sometimes seems dull and grinding. As we live and work in the routine that God has given us, let us do so in the assurance that we live in the City of Refuge, namely in the Lord Jesus Christ. Then let us be sure that our conclusions are based on Scripture, and that we do indeed, as a group of God's people, praise His name.

12
Choose
to Serve God

Joshua 23, 24

There are many illustrations in the Bible of what God has done through older people. We are youth-oriented in America today. But let us never forget the place of the veteran, the experienced and the aged.

The apostle Paul referred to himself in Philemon 9 as Paul the aged. Paul was probably not much more than 60 when he said that. Sixty in that particular time was probably considered "older" than it is today. But I think part of Paul's reason for feeling aged was that the work in which he was engaged had taken its toll. He had poured out his life and strength for the Lord.

Peter was an old man when he said, "So I will always remind you of these things, even though you know them and are firmly established in the truth you now have. I think it is right to refresh your memory as long as I live in the tent of this body, because I know that I will soon put it aside, as our Lord Jesus Christ has made clear to me" (2 Pet. 1:12-14). "I'm going to die. I'm an old man," says

Peter, "but I want to take time to remind you about the things you already know."

Well, Joshua too had some last words. He had some things to say to the leaders of the nation.

As we read Joshua 23, we must remember that years have gone by since Joshua first started to lead the people into the land of Israel. Joshua is an old man and he calls the representatives of the nation together. In that group there are some other old men, men who have stood with Joshua in the battles and have fought with him down through those 20 years and more. They have known what it is to share their understanding and their wisdom in plans and the outworking of those plans in the purposes of God. These are the veterans, men with lined faces and gray hair; these are the desert warriors who have been buffeted about for all that period of time.

I have often thought, not only were the old men there in that council, but there were probably some young men too. These were the young men who were anxious to get on with it. These were some men who were calling for change, and said to Joshua, "We don't do things today as you did in the old days in the desert." I suspect there were some young men who were wondering about their places of leadership—who is going to get the responsibility, who is going to get to press on. They were keenly aware of a passing era as this aged and noble man gave them his valedictory. But the sadness of some of those young men might have been tempered with desire to assume responsibility; because when Joshua passes from the scene, somebody is going to take his place.

So Joshua, this old and honorable man, after 20 years of guidance and direction and marvelous blessing from God, says to young and old alike, "These are the three things you must do; and if you do them you will be blessed of God."

You Must Be Obedient

The first thing you must know to do is to obey. "Be very strong; be careful to obey all that is written in the Book of the Law of Moses" (Josh. 23:6). Personal faith and personal responsibility to the Word of God will guarantee you preservation, spiritual life and a wider influence on those about you.

There is a preserving power in righteousness. The power in righteousness was illustrated when the angel of the Lord came to Abraham and said, "I'm going to wipe out that city." "Oh," said Abraham, "if you could just find 50 men who are righteous, will you save it?" And He said, "All right." And Abraham kept dickering with Him until he finally got it down to only a handful (see Gen. 18:17-33).

God is impressed, if I may put it that way, by the righteousness of a few people. And who knows how much a whole community is affected by those believers who function as salt and light?

In stressing obedience, Joshua was passing on the advice that he himself received earlier. He was told, "Be careful to obey all the law my servant . . . gave you . . . that you may be successful wherever you go" (Josh. 1:7). 1:7). Twenty years later, Joshua is saying, "If you obey and keep the law of God, you will be blessed." He is passing it on.

The Bible teaches us clearly and without any hesitation that obedience is better than sacrifice (see 1 Sam. 15:22). Obedience must be from the heart. Daniel was challenged and tempted, but he said, "I must obey God. I must do what I know is right." Peter said, "We must obey God rather than man." That is what Joshua is saying here in chapter 23, verse 6—you must keep and do all that is written in God's Word. That is a guarantee of spiritual blessing.

You Must Be Set Apart

The second thing Joshua talks about is separation: "Do not associate with these nations that remain among you; do not invoke the names of their gods . . . but . . . hold fast unto the Lord your God" (Josh. 23:7,8). "The Lord your God will drive them out of your way" (Josh. 23:5). He is talking about separation. The Canaanites were dangerous, not as warriors with clubs and spears, but because of the influence they had upon these people. They influenced God's people away from Himself, so God said they were dangerous.

Any person or anything that influences you away from your relationship with God today is a danger. One influence we often refer to is worldliness. We are warned against it. It will lead to apostasy. We need to know what it is to be sanctified, or set apart. We need to know what it is to be purified, or consecrated. We are to be set apart for the glory of God.

You Must Love

Finally, Joshua says, "So be very careful to love the Lord your God" (Josh. 23:11). There was a time for fighting in the experience of these people, but now is the time for love. Here is the key to revival: harmony, peace and unity in the Church of Jesus Christ. This will lift the life of the Church and put us on a new level of experience together.

As you no doubt know, love is the central theme of the

New Testament. Love is best illustrated in the giving of God's Son to save us, but it is also then encouraged as the basic characteristic of the Christian believer. In Romans 5:5, we read, "And hope does not disappoint us, because God has poured out his love into our hearts by the Holy Spirit, whom he has given us." This is a challenge that is put to us on page after page of Scripture.

In many ways it would seem to go beyond even the declaration of truth, although that is of course a primary function of the Christian. This characteristic requires a heart that is filled with love and devotion to the cause of our Saviour. When the Lord asks us to do something, our sense of love will enable us to respond with devotion and commitment. Love is able to lift the truth of God from simple declarations that can be read, and transform them into living experiences.

The Old Testament speaks of the difference between hearts of stone and hearts of flesh. Love is that which makes the difference. So we are to be extremely cautious and careful and as the instruction is given to us in Joshua 23:11, "So be very careful to keep on loving him" *(TLB)*. Or again, as we are instructed in Jude 21, "Keep yourselves in God's love."

These closing instructions from this grand old man of God guarantee our success in Christian living. As we have seen in this chapter, we are called upon to exercise obedience, as seen in verse 6; separation, as seen in verse 7; and love, as described in verse 11. To carefully adhere to these biblical instructions is indeed the guarantee of a successful Christian experience. This is that which will enable us to live a life that is pleasing in the Lord's sight. These characteristics will give us the undergirding of blessing and power that comes only from Him.

Joshua's Moral Power

In the twenty-fourth chapter of the book of Joshua, we read of another speech by Joshua. It starts out somewhat like the first one. But I think it is safe to say that the first speech, in chapter 23, took place in the area called Shiloh, while the second, in chapter 24, took place in the town called Shechem. Chapter 23 seems to be an unofficial rehearsal of the blessing of God, while chapter 24 is the official conference of Joshua as the leader, and the people of Israel as the people of God. Joshua was passing on what God had said to him.

Great moral power is illustrated in both of these speeches, but particularly in chapter 24. These are moving, powerful speeches. They must have drawn attention, response and rapt enthusiasm from the people as they listened to this elder statesman give his valedictory. These were speeches that made a difference because of who Joshua was and what he had done, as well as what he said.

The speech in Joshua 24 was delivered with effectiveness and with influence. Here is a national leader, making a national speech that made a difference. I cannot help but ask, "Where is that power today?" I mean genuine *moral* power, not just a form of rhetoric that inspires and calls forth enthusiasm, but power that moves, shapes and influences.

Where is that power? Mao Tse-tung said, "I'll tell you where it is: power comes from the barrel of a gun." And it does—at least momentarily. But real power originates in other places. It is the moral power Joshua demonstrated in his own life that stood behind his farewell speech. The people listened; they responded to his great, persuasive speech.

There is a theology of leadership in the Bible and that

is the leadership of love. There is leadership in love that enables one to take his proper place of leadership and to get the kind of response from those around him that will enable the work of the gospel to go forward. Jesus set this pattern for us when He said, "I am among you as one who serves" (Luke 22:27). His leadership was based upon His service. That pattern is set for us all. We are to lead in love.

And there is illustrated for us here in Joshua the moral power of a man who is committed to God, who is dependent upon God and who is attempting to serve God in the midst of His people. That man has influence, exercises leadership and will accomplish things for God in love.

God's Grace

As Joshua begins his speech, he immediately points out the grace of God. The Israelites had come to this place at the divine direction of God Himself.

This is an important place in the history of Israel. Years before, Abraham stood in that very same place and God appeared to him and said, "Abraham, I will give this whole country—I will give this whole land to you and to your family that follows." God made that promise in Shechem. Years went by and Abraham's grandson, Jacob, stood there and God repeated the promise. In Joshua 8, Shechem was also the scene of the renewal of the covenant. Shechem is at the very center of the land, and it seems a fitting place for this final address of Joshua. He began by reviewing the past. He told them that God said, "Long ago your forefathers . . . lived beyond the River" (Josh. 24:2), and he reviewed the historical background of the people of God and their relationship to Him.

Joshua reminded the people of God that it was because

of His grace they had come to the place where they now found themselves. That is very important for us to know. Notice that Joshua suddenly said, without any hesitation or apology, "I want to remind you that we've come from a very lowly origin." That is interesting, isn't it? He was giving a patriotic address, a rousing challenge to the people to do the thing that God wants them to do and he said, "I want to remind you we came from very lowly kinds of origins. Our forefathers were idolaters."

Terah, Abraham's father, was an idolater. It is possible that he worshiped the moon. That was the type of thing going on in his time. And it is possible that Abraham himself did the same thing. But for the grace of God, Abraham and his family might have lived and died in their idolatry. But God called Abraham to Himself.

Isaiah, 700 years after Joshua, said to the people, "Look to the rock from which you were cut and to the quarry from which you were hewn" (Isa. 51:1). Great nations have not always been great. Religious people have not always been religious.

Joshua reminded his people of their origin. "You know," he said, "we came from a pretty difficult background. But look what God has done for us." Those blots on the family tree need not hold back an individual. In 1 Corinthians, Paul listed some terrible moral aberrations and said, "The wicked will not inherit the kingdom of God." And then he said a very strange thing: "And that is what some of you were. But you were washed, you were sanctified, you were justified in the name of the Lord Jesus Christ and by the Spirit of our God (1 Cor. 6:9-11). The apostle Paul himself said, "I persecuted the church . . . . But by the grace of God I am what I am, and his grace to me was not without effect" (1 Cor. 15:9,10).

The grace of God changes people, and it gives nations opportunities. The grace of God is operative today. Let it make a new person out of you.

Hudson Taylor came to what he called the exchanged life. He said, "It is not I but Christ. It is not what Hudson Taylor does for God that matters, it is what God does to Hudson Taylor that really counts." That was true for Joshua. That was true for Moses, and Abraham, and it's true for you. You see, God operates in a gracious fashion. The graciousness of God intervenes and rescues us from the things that would ensnare us.

A Word of Warning

Finally, in Joshua's speech there is a word of warning. God, through Joshua, reminded the people, "I sent Moses and Aaron, and I afflicted the Egyptians" (Josh. 24:5). "You saw with your own eyes what I did to the Egyptians" (v. 7). There is a word of warning that we need to observe here: national history is great, but what about national destiny? Nations are judged, just like people. We then, as a nation, are responsible to God. Jeremiah said, "When he is angry, the earth trembles; the nations cannot endure his wrath" (Jer. 10:10).

We have a great heritage in this country, but we have lost our way because we have gone our way and not God's way. It is our neglect of God and His commandments that is our own undoing. That is what Joshua is warning about in this chapter. America is currently in the place of judgment, the divine judgment of God. We need to awaken before it is too late. National history is a magnificent way to trace the hand of God. But national destiny is dependent upon obedience to God.

Nations are judged, just as people are judged and are

responsible to God. Many portions of Scripture bring this to our attention. The psalmist suggested, "He *is* the governor among the nations" (Ps. 22:28, *KJV*). God is referred to as the King of all the earth. We are responsible to Him. We have been warned by many that indeed we have lost our way and the problem is that we are lost because it is our way and not God's way.

Historians point out that nations have fallen, either to the ravages of time and ultimate extinction, or they have simply taken a place far down on the scale of importance. Men point out how the whole unfolding of history illustrates the nature and activity of God. If a nation is disobedient to God and to His purposes, that nation will ultimately fall. When moral chaos sets in upon a society, it stands on the brink of destruction. Our neglect of God and His commandments will be the undoing of this nation, unless we repent and turn to Him.

There was an advertisement that appeared in a public journal some time ago, sponsored by Tiffany & Co. This was not an advertisement for jewelry, but one that asked a question that can be condensed in the following way: Is *inflation* the real problem? This legendary luxury store went on to suggest that inflation is simply the inevitable, final result of our follies which include forsaking our religious heritage, not only in our schools, but everywhere, thus accentuating crime, immorality, greed and selfishness.

God has given us opportunity after opportunity and we are grateful for those additional evidences of His grace. Let us indeed awaken as a nation so that we may continue to expect the blessings of the Lord.

A Covenant Relationship

Joshua challenged the people of his day to decide

whether they were going to serve the Lord God or the gods their forefathers served. And today, we are faced with this same challenge. Will we serve the Lord God or the gods of this world?

We do not talk much about covenants today. It is an old-fashioned word. We talk about testaments or agreements or pacts. But the covenant that is spoken of in the Bible has many different meanings. God wants to exist between Himself and His people—the covenant relationship. And this is where the question of choice comes in. You have heard it said that Christianity is only one generation from extinction; consequently we need to be reminded of the truth, and we need to hold it before people so they might have the opportunity to make their choice.

If we are not held steady in this covenant relationship, we tend to drift. The book that follows Joshua, the book of Judges, is the story of drift. The people of God stayed solid and true for awhile. Joshua 24:31 says, "Israel served the Lord throughout the lifetime of Joshua and of the elders who outlived him and who had experienced everything the Lord had done for Israel." That is a fine testimony, and it shows the influence of Joshua upon the generation in which he lived. But it is not such a happy story in the next book, for there we begin to see that people drifted away from God.

We see this again and again in the Bible. The book of Revelation talks about the church at Ephesus. God's condemnation of that church was this: you have left your first love, you are out of fellowship with the Lord. The condemnation leveled against the church of Laodicea was this: you are neither hot nor cold, you have moved away from your commitment to God.

If we were to look at the history of the covenant concept in the Bible we could spend a long time. Men have always made pacts between themselves. Sometimes they were sealed in blood. In the covenant between God and His people, God has graciously taken the initiative. God offers in a covenant relationship His own fellowship with man. God makes promises to His people. Some of those promises are conditional, based upon human obedience.

God made a covenant with Noah that He would not destroy the earth by flood again (see Gen. 9:11). God made a covenant with Abraham, in which God established a special relationship with Abraham (see Gen. 12:1-3). Later God made a covenant with the nation of Israel (see Exod. 19:3-8). This covenant was ratified by a sacrifice and by sprinkling with blood so that the people had it clearly in their minds. God said, "You'll be my people if you'll do certain things." The people said, "All right, we'll be your people; and to prove this, we'll ratify this covenant by the ritual you have commanded" (see Exod. 24:3-8). The nation of Israel was identified as the people of God through this covenant relationship. Promises were given for obedience and penalties were held forth for disobedience.

So long as the people of God obeyed God, they experienced His promises and His blessing. When they drifted away from that covenant relationship of obedience to God, they came under His judgment. It is still true today.

Rebellion Forfeits the Covenant

Another truth that springs at us here is though the nation had achieved this covenant relationship with God, an individual might forfeit his rights by deliberate rebellion against God. Then he was no longer counted as part of that covenant relationship. He was considered to be, in the language of the Old Testament, cut off from God's people.

Joshua was largely concerned about idolatry, for he was surrounded by it. That influence is always there; and we, as well as the people in Joshua's day, are warned against it. Calvin spoke of the human mind as an idol manufacturing machine. We are all subject to that. It is natural for us to create idols. Riches will do that; not only riches of money, but riches of all kinds. We may idolize an unusually gifted personality, the riches of intellect or the riches of a stable emotional life.

The aged apostle John, knowing the tendency of the human heart to depart from God, said, "Dear children, keep yourselves from idols" (1 John 5:21).

This is what Joshua was concerned about, and he warned the people. He said, "You've got to choose; because if you don't serve the Lord God Jehovah, you'll serve some idol." What are your idols? Goals, ambitions, accomplishments? All of these can become idols. Even people can become idols.

Henry Ward Beecher, a great American preacher, visited Boston one time. The people packed the church where he was going to preach. But because of some delay in his travel, he did not arrive. So his brother, Edward Beecher, got up to preach. And people all over the congregation began to get up and walk out. Dr. Beecher stopped the service and said, "Wait a minute. If you've come here to hear Henry Ward Beecher, go on; but if you've come here to worship God, sit down and worship."

It is possible to let people assume a prominence in our lives that borders on idolatry. Idols are dangerous; idols are attractive. It is all too easy to drift into idolatry.

But God does not sit idly by while we drift. According to Jeremiah, God said to His people, "I will not give you up—I will plead for you to return to me, and will keep on pleading; yes, even with your children's children in the years to come! Look around you and see if you can find another nation anywhere that has traded in its old gods for new ones—even though their gods are nothing. Send to the west to the island of Cyprus; send to the east to the deserts of Kedar. See if anyone there has ever heard so strange a thing as this. And yet my people have given up their glorious God for silly idols! The heavens are shocked at such a thing and shrink back in horror and dismay. For my people have done two evil things: They have forsaken me, the Fountain of Life-giving Water; and they have built for themselves broken cisterns that can't hold water!" (Jer. 2:9-13, *TLB*).

Who Will You Serve?

We must choose whom we are going to serve. And there is only one reasonable choice: The God of power, the God who leads His people from bondage, the God who leads and protects and provides for His people year after year after year.

Whom will you serve? One of God's servants, faced with that question, said, "Lord, to whom shall we go? You have the words of eternal life" (John 6:68). There are no other gods to choose; there is no other way.

There is only one response to this kind of question: "Far be it from us to forsake the LORD to serve other gods! It was the LORD our God himself who brought us and our forefathers up out of Egypt, from that land of slavery, and performed those great signs before our eyes. He pro-

147

tected us on our entire journey and among all the nations through which we traveled" (Josh. 24:16,17).

We must not only choose God, we must obey Him. "The people said to Joshua, 'We will serve the LORD our God and obey him'" (Josh. 24:24). There is no higher point in all of the Old Testament in response to the purposes of God. There will be no higher point in your life, and there is no greater kind of commitment than that found in that verse. We will serve the Lord and obey Him. That is how you choose God; that's how you make your choice in terms of the great conflicts of our day.

Paul tells us that we are not our own, "You were bought at a price. Therefore honor God" (1 Cor. 6:20). As you reflect on the love of God you will be drawn to Him, for Jesus said, "But I, when I am lifted up from the earth, will draw all men to myself" (John 12:32).

In Greek mythology there's a story about Odysseus, who sailed past the island of the sirens. The sirens had the power to charm all who listened to their singing, and thus lure them to their destruction. Odysseus wanted to hear the sirens' song without endangering himself and his crew, so he filled the ears of his crew with wax and had them bind him to the mast. Thus, they safely passed that fatal place.

But there's another story in Greek mythology. Orpheus went with the Argonauts to search for the golden fleece. When they sailed by the sirens' island, Orpheus played better music than the sirens; he enchanted the crew with a superior melody and they passed safely by.

God does not keep you from hearing about other gods. He will not bind you by force. But He does make better music. And He asks you to choose for yourself. If you do not choose Him, it is because you've closed your eyes to

His person. You have stopped your ears from hearing His gracious words.

Joshua said, "Then choose for yourselves this day whom you will serve." And the people said, "We too will serve the Lord, because he is our God" (Josh. 24:15,18).

The Holiness of God

The book of Joshua began with a funeral and ends with three funerals. It began with a review of what God had promised and closes with the renewal of the covenant. In the closing verses of this book we can see an emphasis on the character of God, the character of Joshua and the conclusion of an era.

Joshua, in his last great speech to the people, appealed to them to remember all the covenant of God. And he gave them the great, heart-warming invitation to choose to serve God. The people said, "All right, we're with you, Joshua. You're right. God has been marvelous, God has been wonderful, we will serve Him."

And then strangely enough, Joshua said, "You are not able to serve the LORD. He is a holy God; He is a jealous God. He will not forgive your rebellion and your sins" (Josh. 24:19).

I think Joshua was provoking or testing the people. They said, "We will serve the Lord." And Joshua said, "You can't serve God. Why? God is holy. How do you expect to serve God, when He's so holy?" I think Joshua is really saying, "Do you really know what you're saying? Don't be quick and shallow and superficial about your promises to God for He is holy."

God Is Holy

What does holy mean? We do not know much about

149

holiness, so we rarely use the word. If we do use it in our everyday language, it is usually in a caricature.

To really understand the holiness of God is highly demanding; it takes intensive study of Scripture. The holiness of God calls for people to fall down before Him. God is not just a better model of the idols around us. God is not just the "man upstairs," the unknown force and power of the universe; He is God, the holy One in whose presence no person can stand.

Isaiah said of Him, "I saw the LORD seated on a throne, high and exalted" and the seraphim cried one to another, "Holy, holy, holy, is the LORD Almighty; the whole earth is full of his glory" (Isa. 6:1,3).

It is no wonder, then when we pray, we say, "Our Father in heaven, hallowed [holy] be your name" (Matt. 6:9). Jesus, in the New Testament, is referred to as the holy One and the Just. Jeremiah, when he was talking about God, said he was overcome. He said, "My heart is broken within me; all my bones tremble . . . because of the LORD and his holy words" (Jer. 23:9).

Have you ever been staggered by the holiness of God? Now I know there are facets of God's character that we constantly need to review in the Bible. I know that God is pictured as a father, and that "As a father has compassion on his children, so the LORD has compassion on those who fear him" (Ps. 103:13). He remembers our frame, He knows that we are dust (see Ps. 103:14). There is that family relationship and I thank God for that. I think we need, however, never to get away from one of the great attributes of God as described by Scripture: that He is holy.

It seems to me that Joshua is saying to the people,

"Wait a minute. You cannot serve the Lord. He's holy, He's a jealous God. Be sure you understand what you're saying and what you're doing before you glibly commit yourselves. Be careful what you say, for God is holy. Be careful what you do, for God is holy."

Our only hope in the face of the holy God is a God who is merciful. The Saviour says, "Come to me, all you who are weary and burdened, and I will give you rest" (Matt. 11:28). He is pictured for us in the book of Revelation as standing at the door and knocking; if you will open the door, He will come in (see Rev. 3:20). That is true. But Scripture also teaches us that we must want to have this relationship with all of our heart and not superficially, but with a deep, all-encompassing commitment to Jesus Christ.

In the New Testament, Jesus told the young lawyer, "Go, sell your possessions and give to the poor . . . . Then come, follow me" (Matt. 19:21). A scribe came one time to Jesus and said, "Master, I've been listening to what you have to say. I'll do anything for you, I'll go anywhere that you want me to go." Jesus said, "Wait a minute. You see the birds that fly through the air? They have nests to go into. You see the foxes that run across the field? They have holes in the ground they can go to. But I have no place to eat or to put my head. Are you sure you want to follow me?" (see Matt. 8:19,20).

What about the apostle Paul? God struck him down with a thunderbolt one day, and he picked himself up out of the dust in the desert and said, "Lord, what do you want me to do?" And one of his first messages concerned how much he had to suffer because he was going to be Christ's servant (see Acts 9:1-6,16). Trial is no sign that God does not love us.

The Character of Joshua

The character of God centers in holiness. And He demands holiness on the part of His people. Then you see the character of Joshua in Joshua 24:29,30. Joshua died and was buried at the border of his inheritance. Here was a man who lived under almost constant tension and excitement from the very earliest days of his life. He led that venture into the land, the people in their first battle and he was chosen to succeed Moses. He spent a lifetime in conflict with the enemy and in leadership of an often rebellious people. And yet there is no word of direct blame recorded against Joshua. There are a couple of hints and intimations in a place or two that Joshua did not wait as long as he should in seeking the mind of God. But basically there is no blaming of Joshua for any factor in his life.

It is no wonder to me that many consider Joshua prefigures the greater Joshua, the Lord Jesus Christ. Here is a man who is never accused of self-seeking. He has a strong will, but that will is committed to God. He exhibits unquestioning obedience to God's commands. His life is a constant, glowing experience right up until his death.

In these farewell speeches, we see spiritual insight and genuine pious concern on the part of the speaker. This warrior saint knew God's promises years before, back in the early days of this book. The promise that came to Joshua must have stood by him through thick and thin, night and day, through all the battles and all the trials and temptations. God said to him, "As I was with Moses, so I will be with you" (Josh. 1:5). Joshua accepted that, he believed it and he acted accordingly.

The character of Joshua, I believe, centers in this one fact: he had a God-centered experience. That is what God asks of you and me. That is the purpose of our studying and

152

trying to dig in and find out more and more about the pattern God has for us here. Joshua had his ups and downs; he had his problems. His was not an easy smooth-flowing kind of life by any means. But at the end of his life, at his funeral, there is no blame attached to him in any way. That is a remarkable testimony, and it is the testimony toward which we ought to be aiming in our own experience.

Conclusion of an Era

Joshua's funeral marks the end of an era. But there are three funerals. One was Joshua's. Another one was Joseph's. Did it strike you as unusual when you read about the bones of Joseph here at the end of the book of Joshua? Joseph died many generations before this; so how does he get into the scene now? When Joseph was dying down in Egypt, he made the people agree to keep his bones and not put him into a permanent grave until his people were in their permanent land (see Gen. 50:25). And so the era comes to a close, God once again proved Himself to be exactly what He said He would be, trustworthy,

The third funeral was Eleazar's. He was the son of Aaron. He appears to have served well and faithfully. Some see in these three people the shadow of the coming Saviour. Joseph His prophet, Eleazar the faithful priest and Joshua the ruler of the host of Israel, the king. Prophet, priest and king.

These were giants of the faith, but now they are gone. These three funerals wipe out some of the great leadership so far as Israel is concerned. But this fact remains: though people come and go, God remains faithful. That, I believe, is the theme and the thrust of this book. God is faithful; you can trust Him; He will not let you down. Our Lord is the same yesterday, today and forever.

153